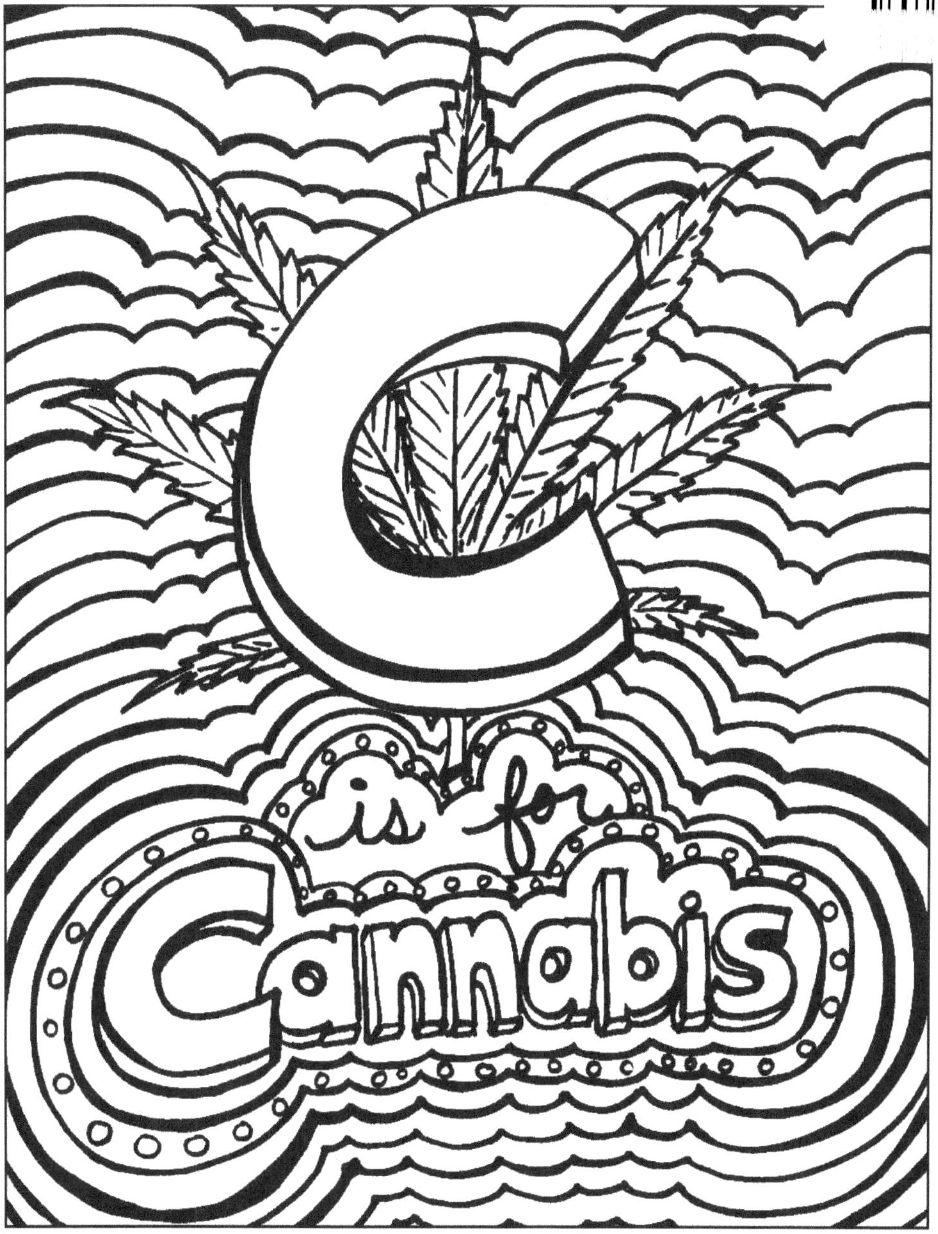

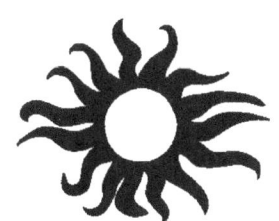

C is for Cannabis

The Coloring Book

By Carolynn Schwartz, aka SoulMama

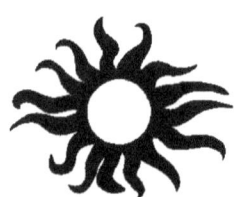

Dedication

This book is dedicated to all the weed smokin' mamas out there – you know who you are.

Thank you

Thank you to Mother Nature for giving us the most incredible gift of all – Cannabis!

About The Author

Carolynn Schwartz, aka Carolynn Schwartz Black, aka Carolynn Black, aka SoulMama is many things. In addition to a coloring book creator and graphic artist, I am a wife, mother, singer/songwriter, crooner, Music Together® teacher, event planner, blogger, activist, voice-over artist, and general Jill of all trades. I have fronted bands in Madison, WI for the last 14 years or so, and in my native NYC for the decade before that.

As you may have guessed by the title and contents of this book, I enjoy cannabis. My first time smoking pot was way back in 1985 while on summer vacation with friends on Cape Cod (Hey Janet! Hey Gillian!). I don't remember much about it and I wish I could say it was magical and changed my life, but I was only 15 and it would be several years before I had the nerve to buy any weed for myself. I spent my 20's having all kinds of fun (before the internet made everything permanent) and smoking pot was just part of the party. Somewhere in my early 30's I became a daily smoker when I figured out that it complements my antidepressant. Flash forward to 2019 and I'm a weed smokin' mama, loud and proud.

Check out my other coloring books on Amazon.com:

- Interesting Insults & Creative Curses for Adults to Color Volume 1
- Interesting Insults & Creative Curses for Adults to Color Volume 2
- Interesting Insults & Creative Curses for Adults to Color Volume 3, The Abecedarium
- I Adulted Today and other Delightful Doodles
- I am allowed to be human & other positive affirmations from Coach Me Dave
- Pantsuit Nation: The Coloring Book
- We Will Not Be Silent: Signs from The Women's March
- Give The Drummer Some: The Clyde Stubblefield Coloring Book
- A is for Awesome: A Positive Alphabet Primer
- Girls Rock Camp: a fundraiser for Girls Rock Camp Madison

All of the above books are also available to purchase in physical form or to download from my Etsy shop, along with tote bags, t-shirts, greeting cards, postcards, stickers, a gazillion individual downloadable coloring pages. WARNING: Some of my designs are R-Rated, as in swear words and vulgar language. No dirty pictures except for the ones in your mind. Many of my designs are snarky, and some are empowering. Download a bunch, invite some friends, toke up, and have a party!

www.etsy.com/shop/SoulMamasStuff
www.soulmamasays.wordpress.com
www.facebook.com/soulmamasstuff
www.facebook.com/2Broads1Band
www.soundcloud.com/carolynn-schwartz-black
www.store.cdbaby.com/cd/carolynnchwartzblack
Instagram: @SoulMamasStuff   Twitter: @SoulMamaSays

Contents

About This Book

Cannabis, Hemp, Marijuana, Whacky Tobacky, Weed, whatever you want to call it, has so much more to offer us than what most people think. People have been using it for its medicinal properties for a very long time and will continue to do so as its benefits become more widely researched and made legal and available. Don't get me wrong, getting high is awesome and sometimes you just want to get out of your head for whatever reason. It's just that there are so many things that can be treated with cannabis in its various forms including anxiety, depression, PTSD, chronic pain, epilepsy, multiple sclerosis, glaucoma, cancer, arthritis, Crohn's Disease, Parkinson's Disease, and Alzheimers. It can also be used as a digestive aid or an appetite stimulant. Many people are making the switch from opioids to cannabis as medical marijuana becomes available and legal in many states. The more that this can happen, the better.

Personally, I smoke daily to complement my daily antidepressant. Depending upon the strain, it can have a calming effect on me that allows me to be present in the moment when I am feeling too naturally amped up (impatient, hyper, angry), or perhaps a stimulating, focusing effect that can help with creative work or chores that need to be done. One thing is for sure, different strains have different effects on different people. Unfortunately, because it is still illegal in many places, there are many perfectly wonderful human beings hiding in the shadows. Hopefully, as recreational legalization makes its way across the country the stigma associated with smoking cannabis will fade into history.

The words I chose to doodle and draw in this book were elicited from my own mind, my friends, google searches, and a couple private stoner mommy Facebook groups. You know who you are! If you're not sure what something is, look it up!

I hope you enjoy this book as much as I did creating it. Just coloring has been shown to have similar benefits to meditation, I get the same from drawing these designs. It is a mindful practice and in the end I have something beautiful to share. If you are so inclined, please take a picture of your colored creation and send it to me at Soulmamasstuff@gmail.com or share it on my facebook page.

Happy Coloring!

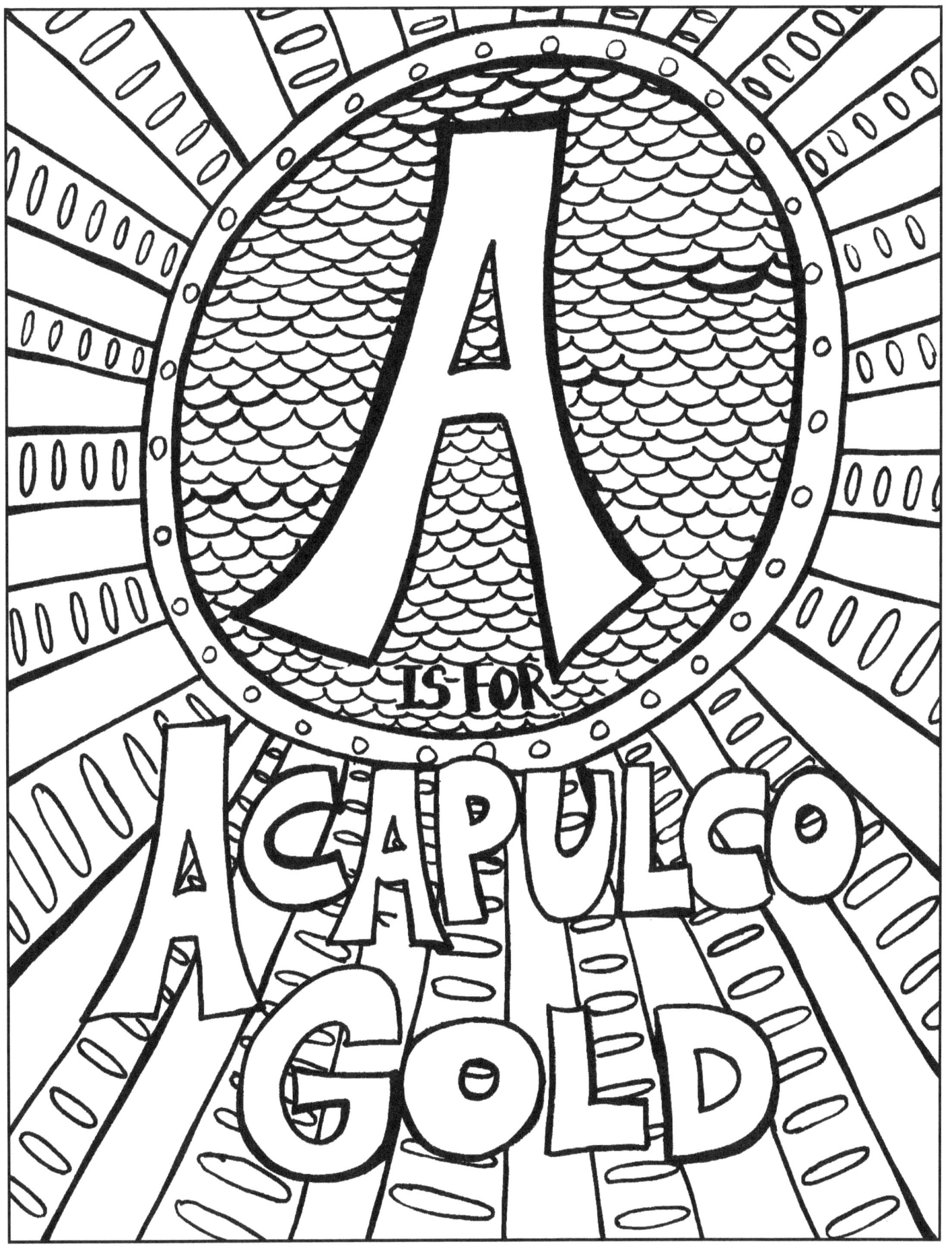

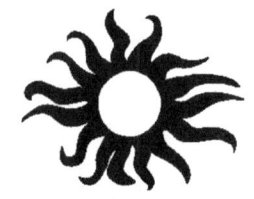

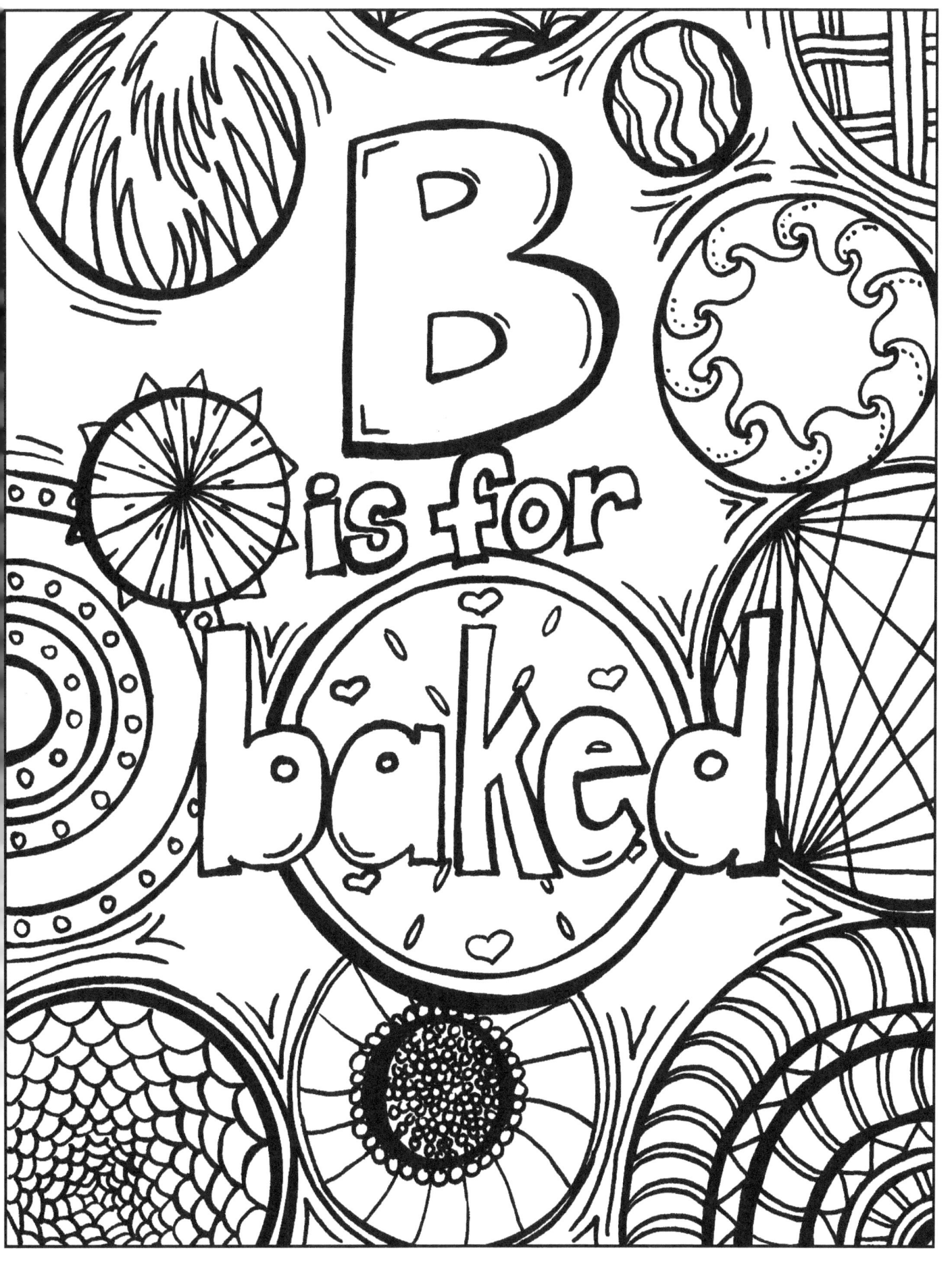

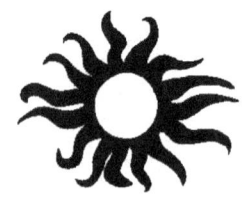

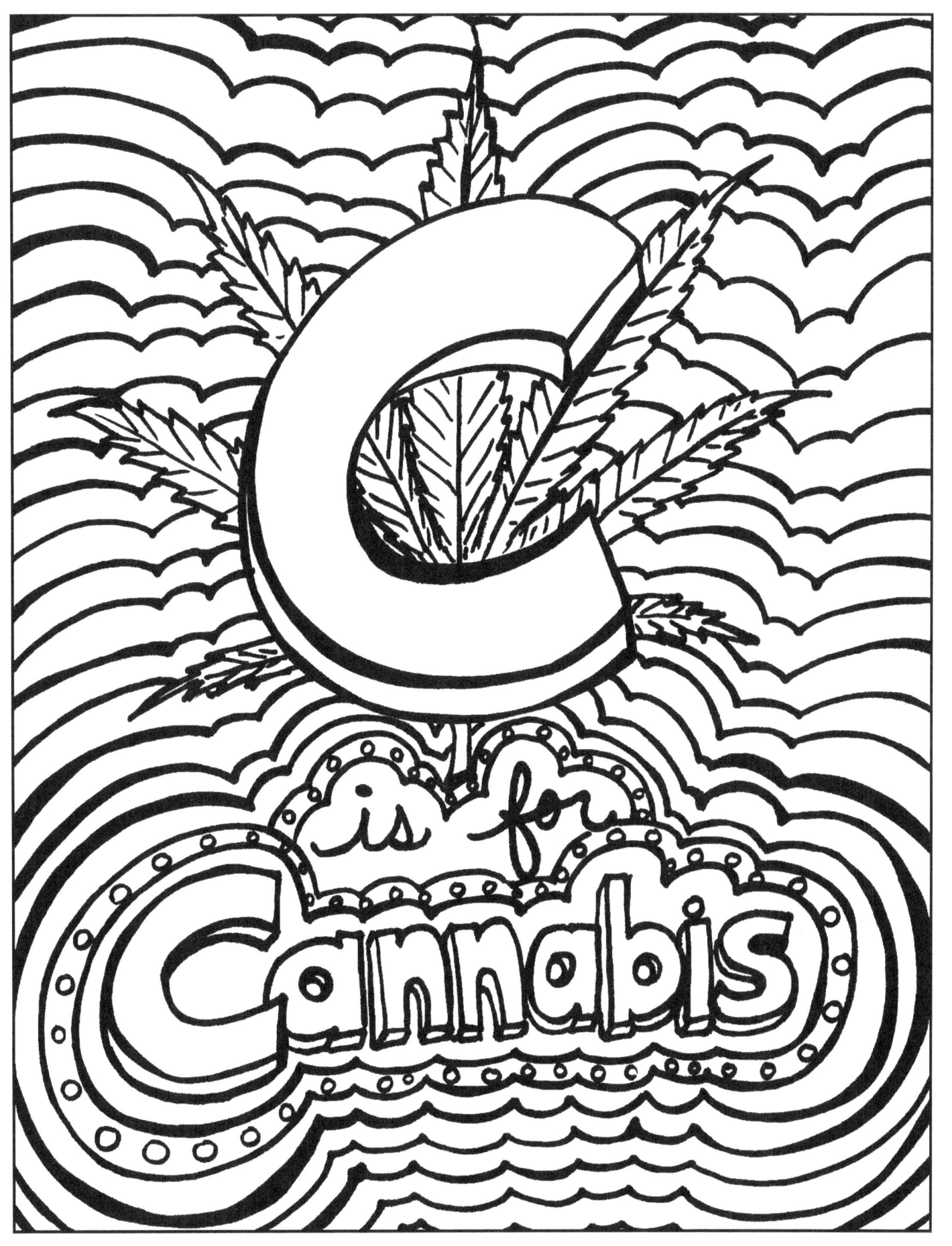

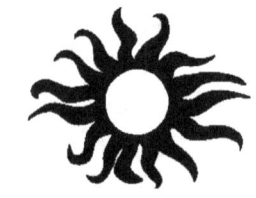

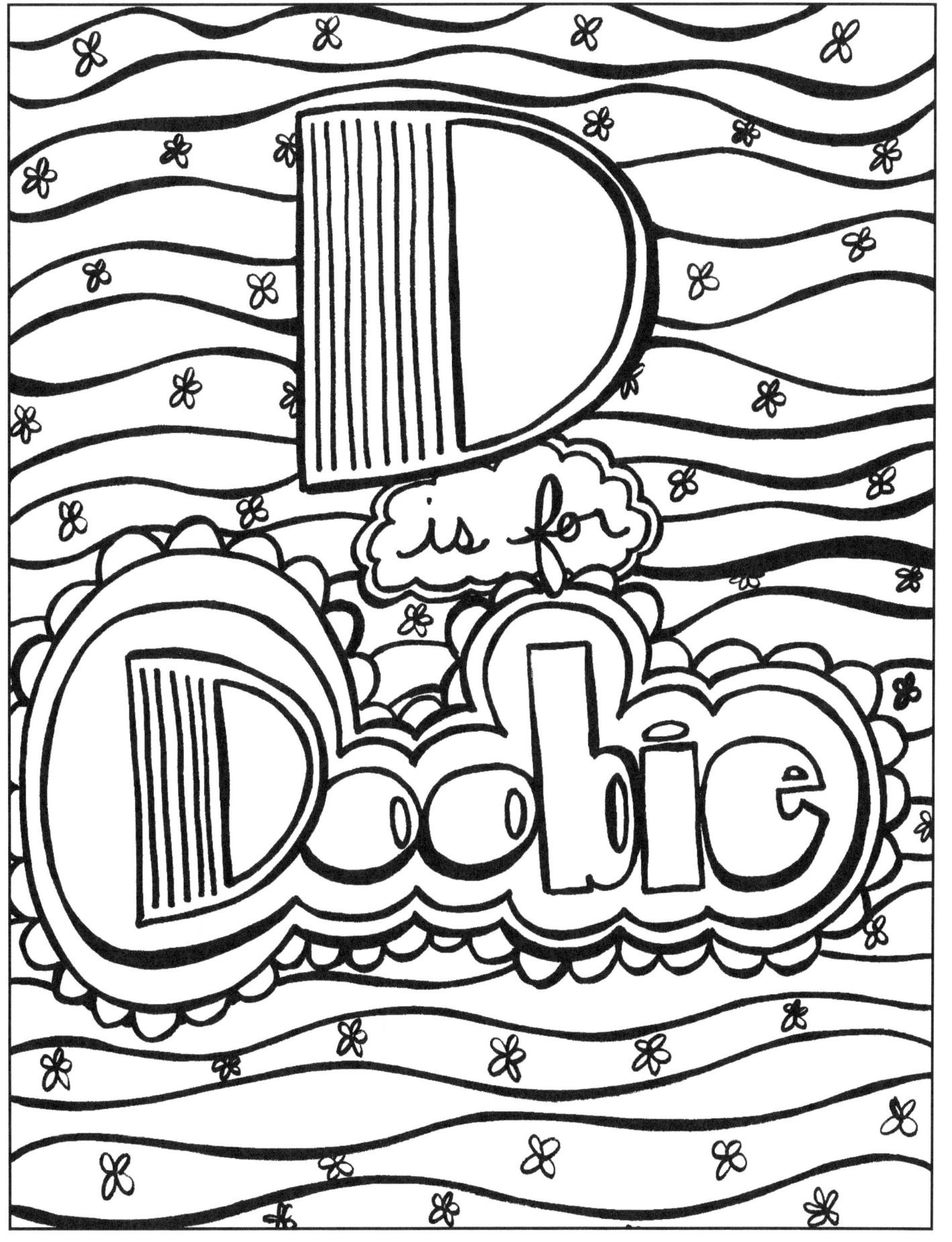

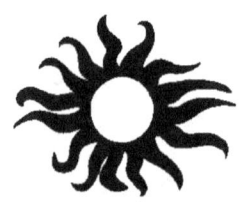

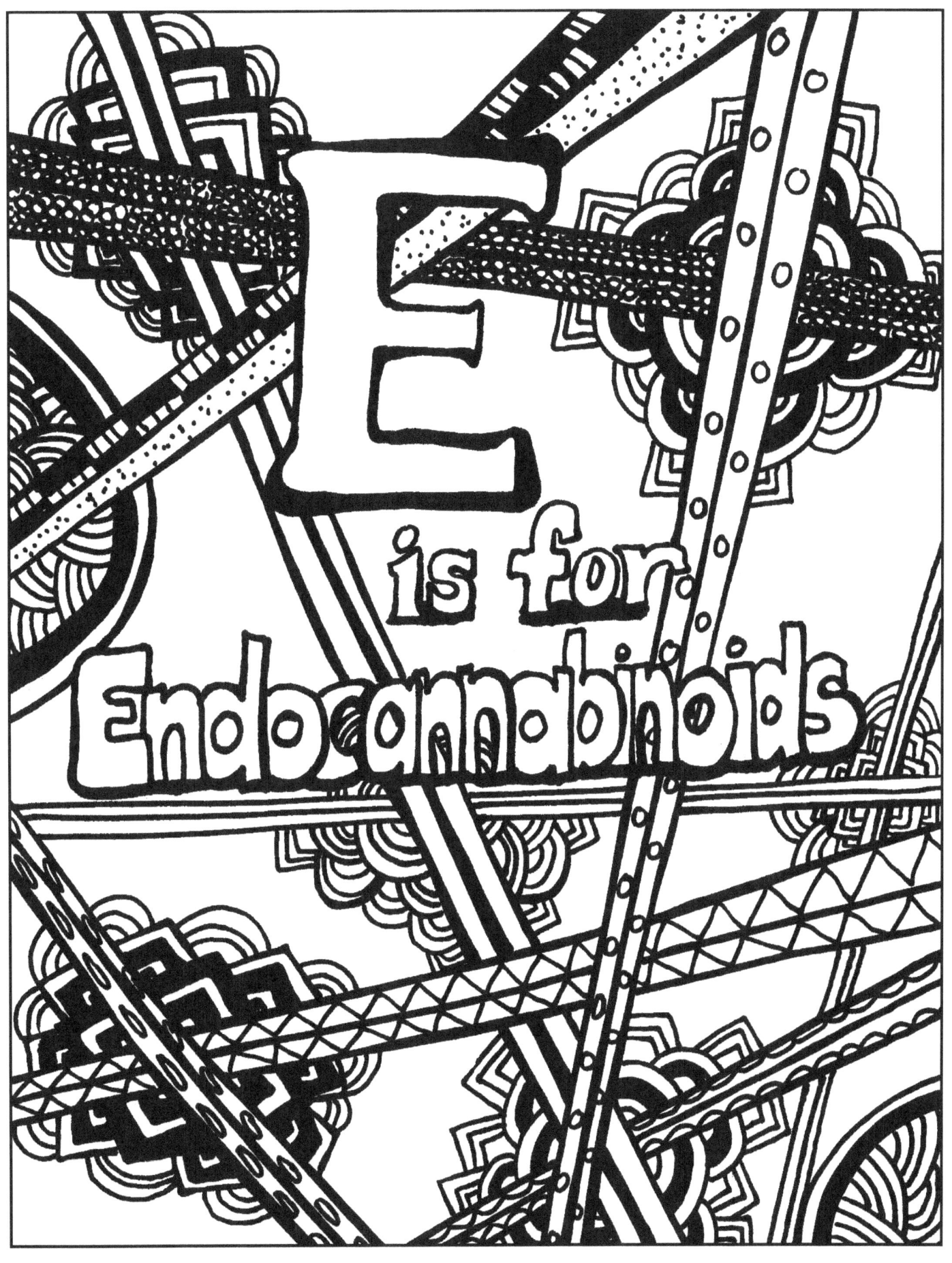

E is for Endocannabinoids

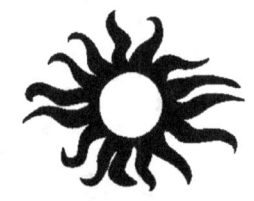

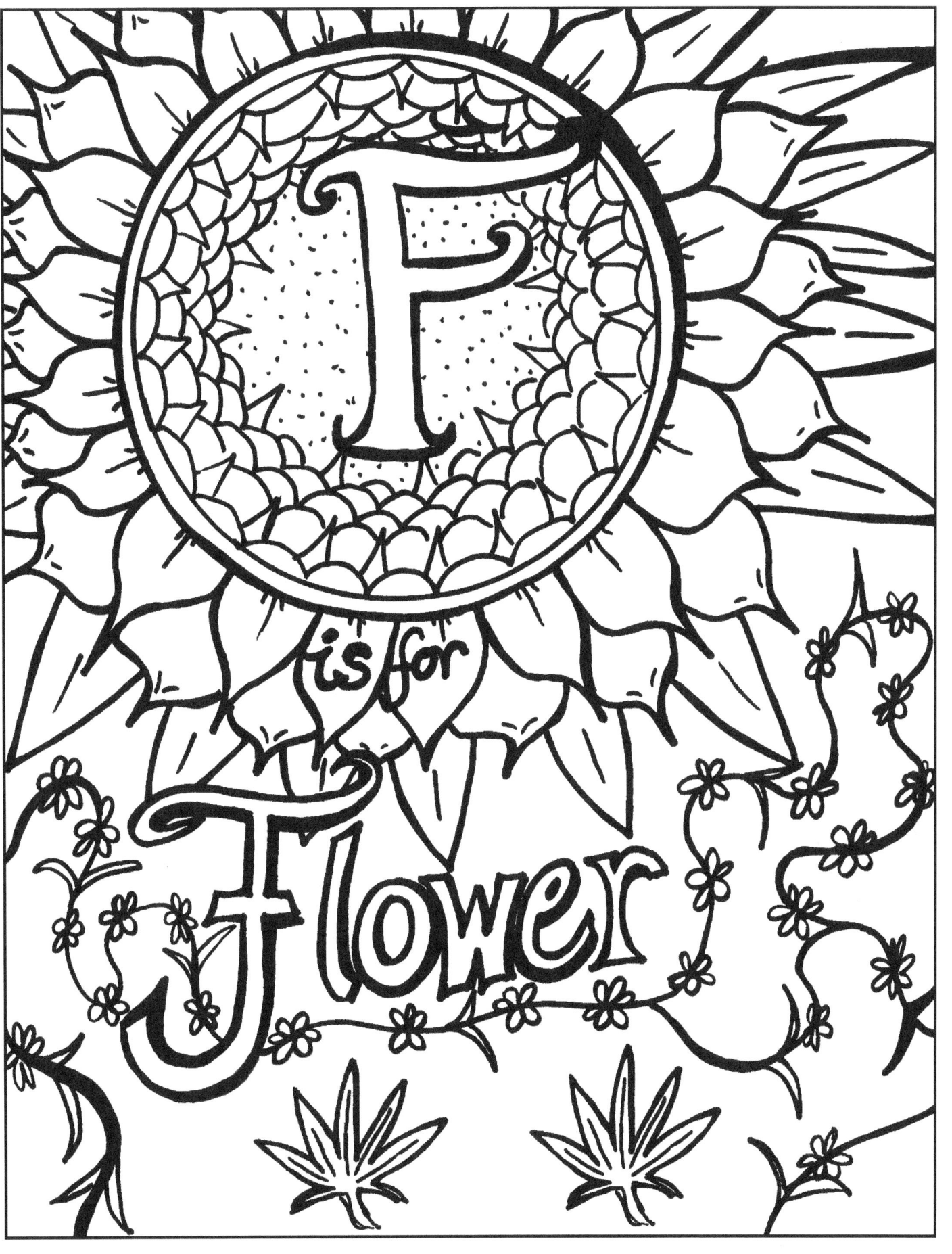

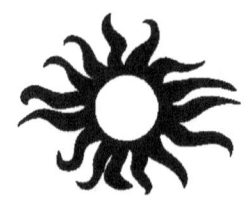

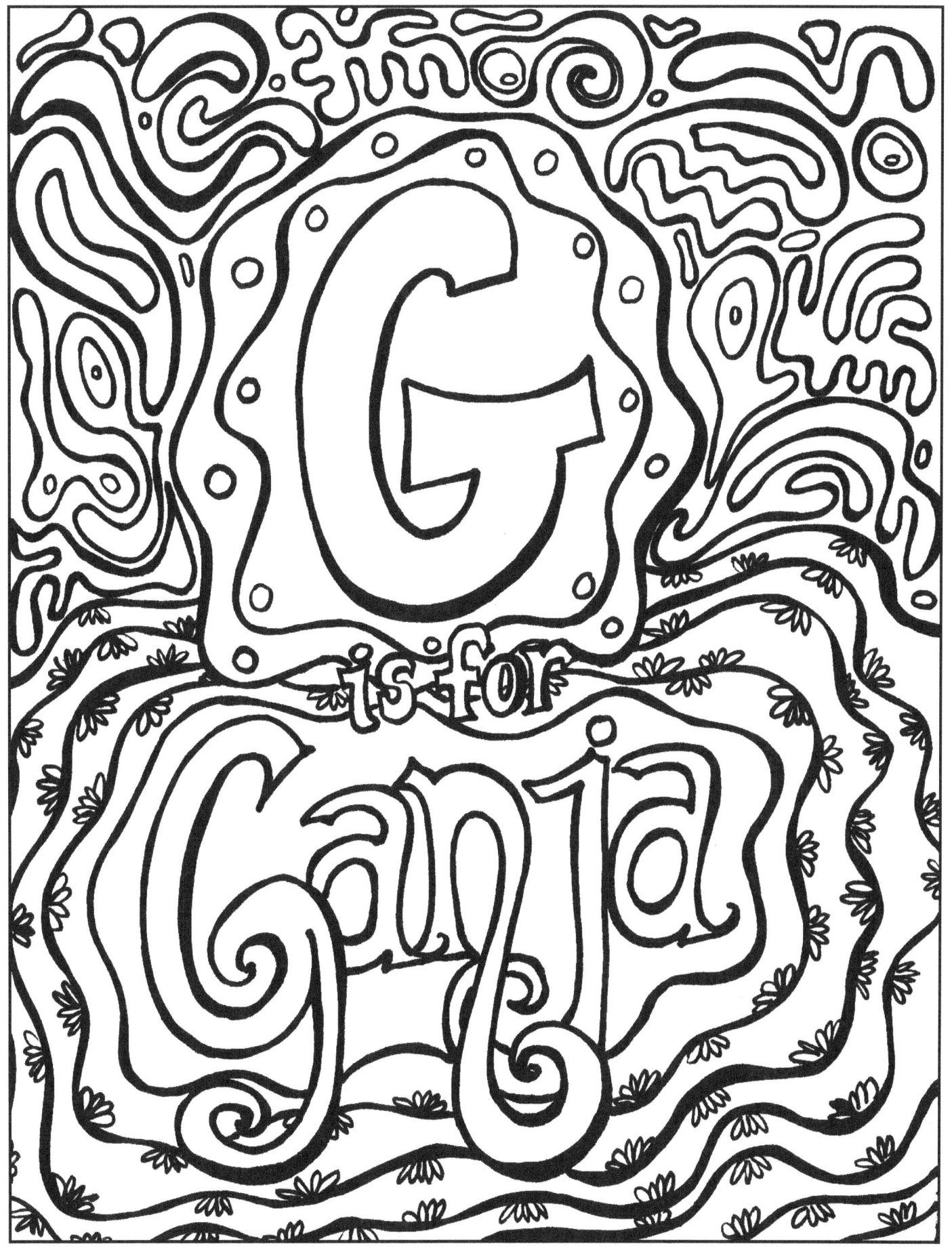

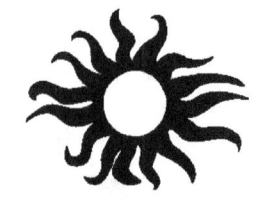

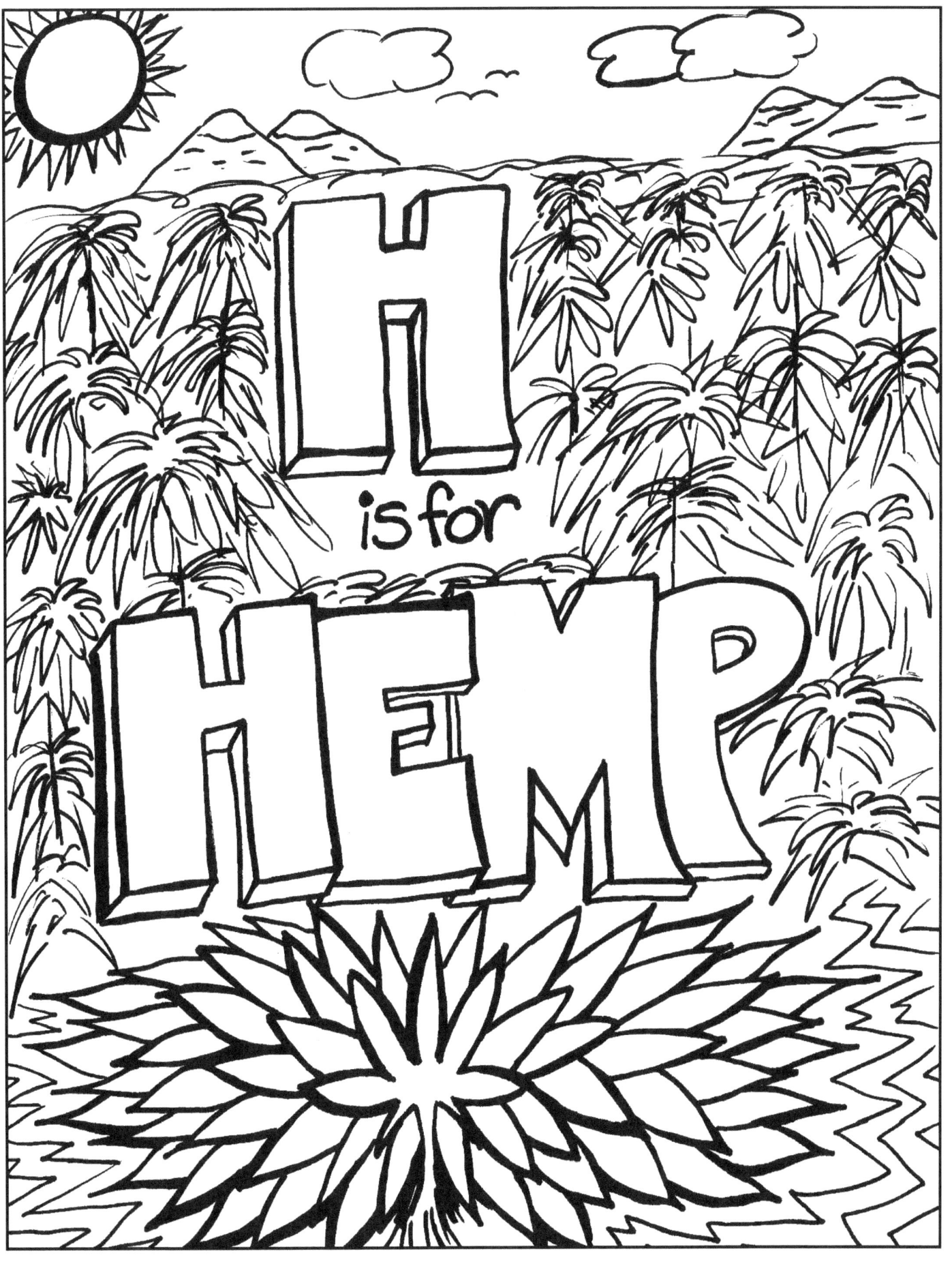

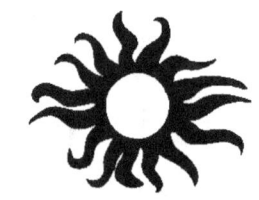

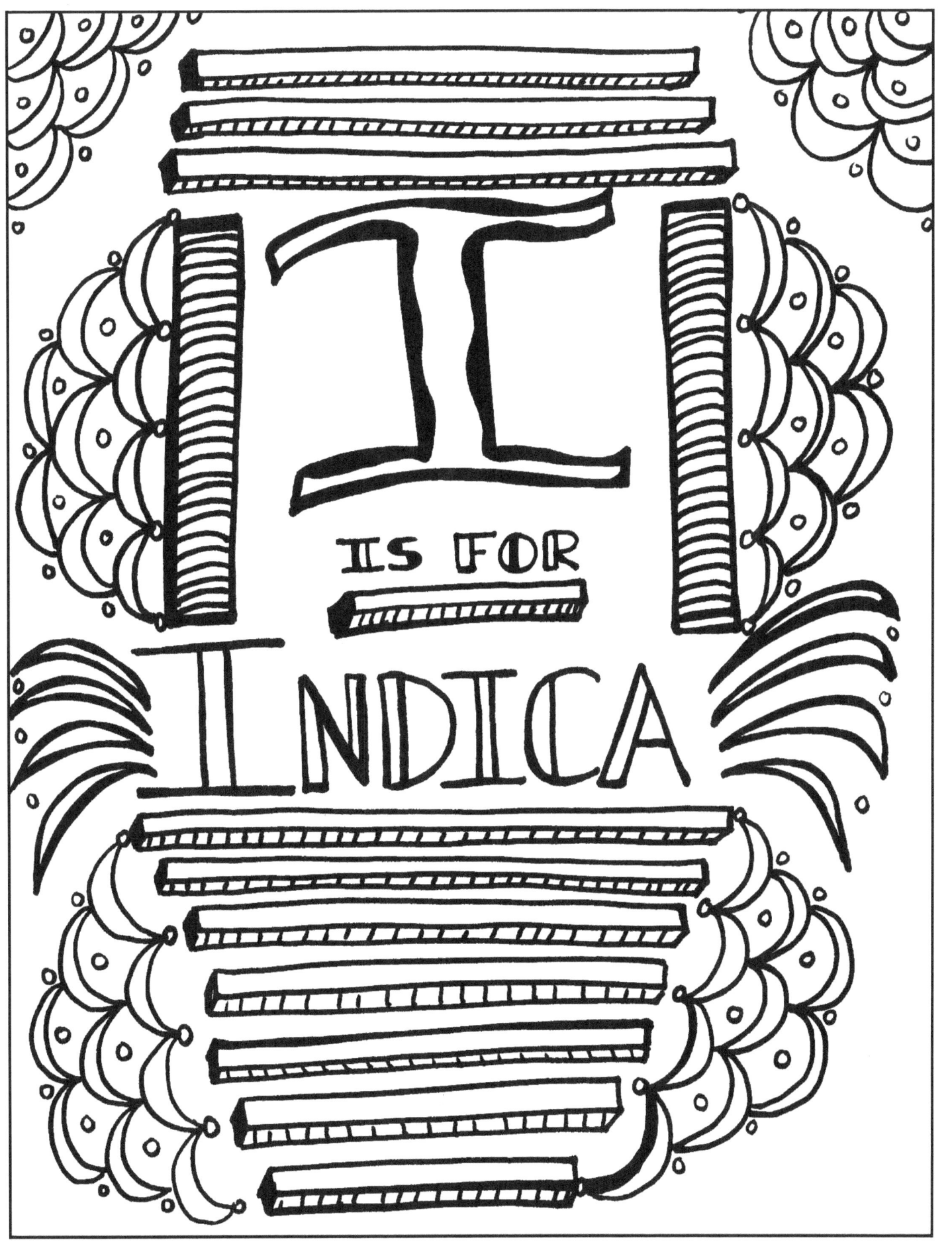

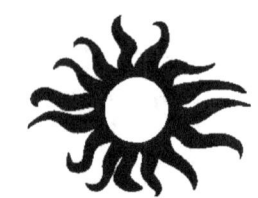

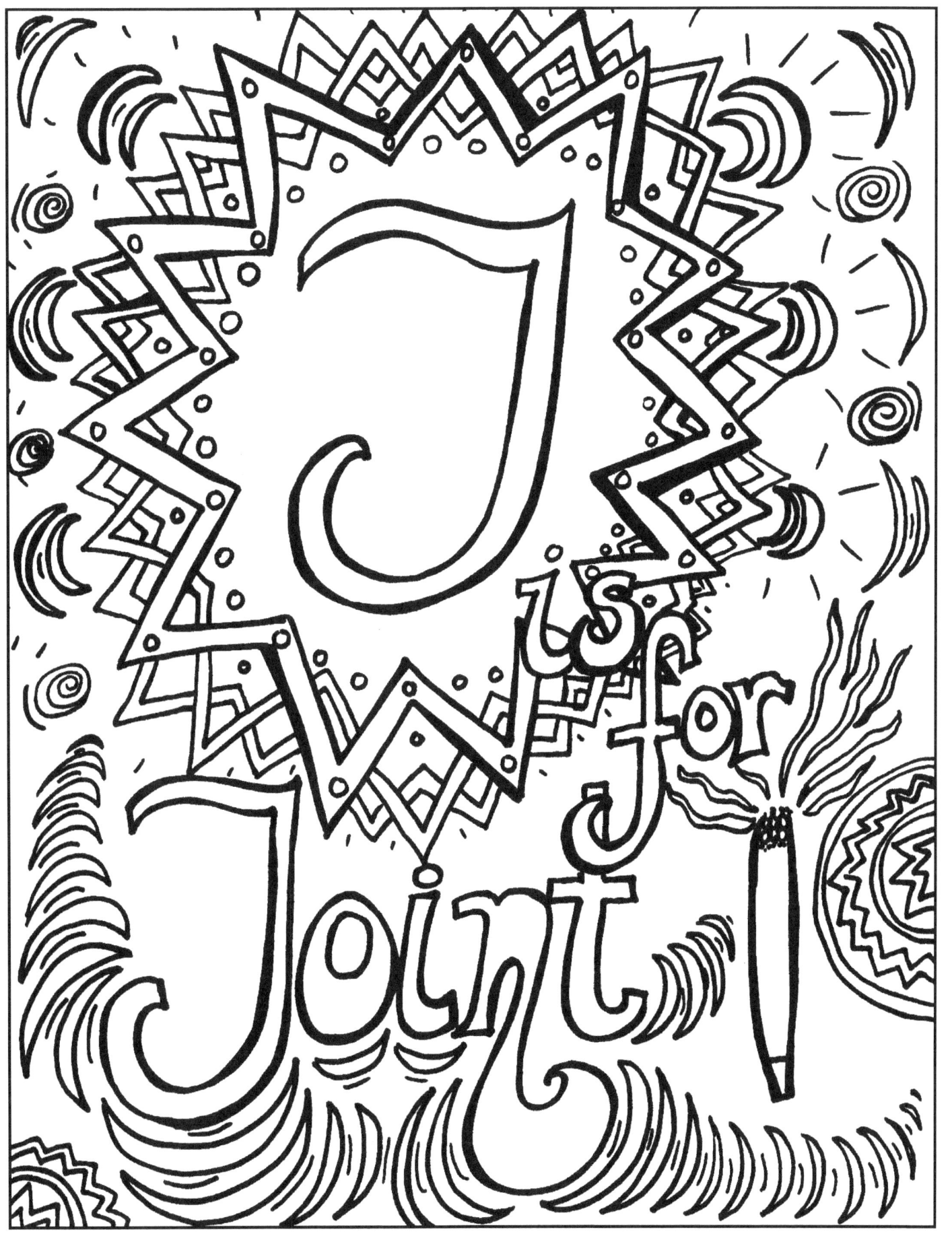

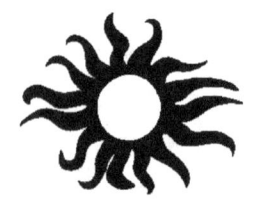

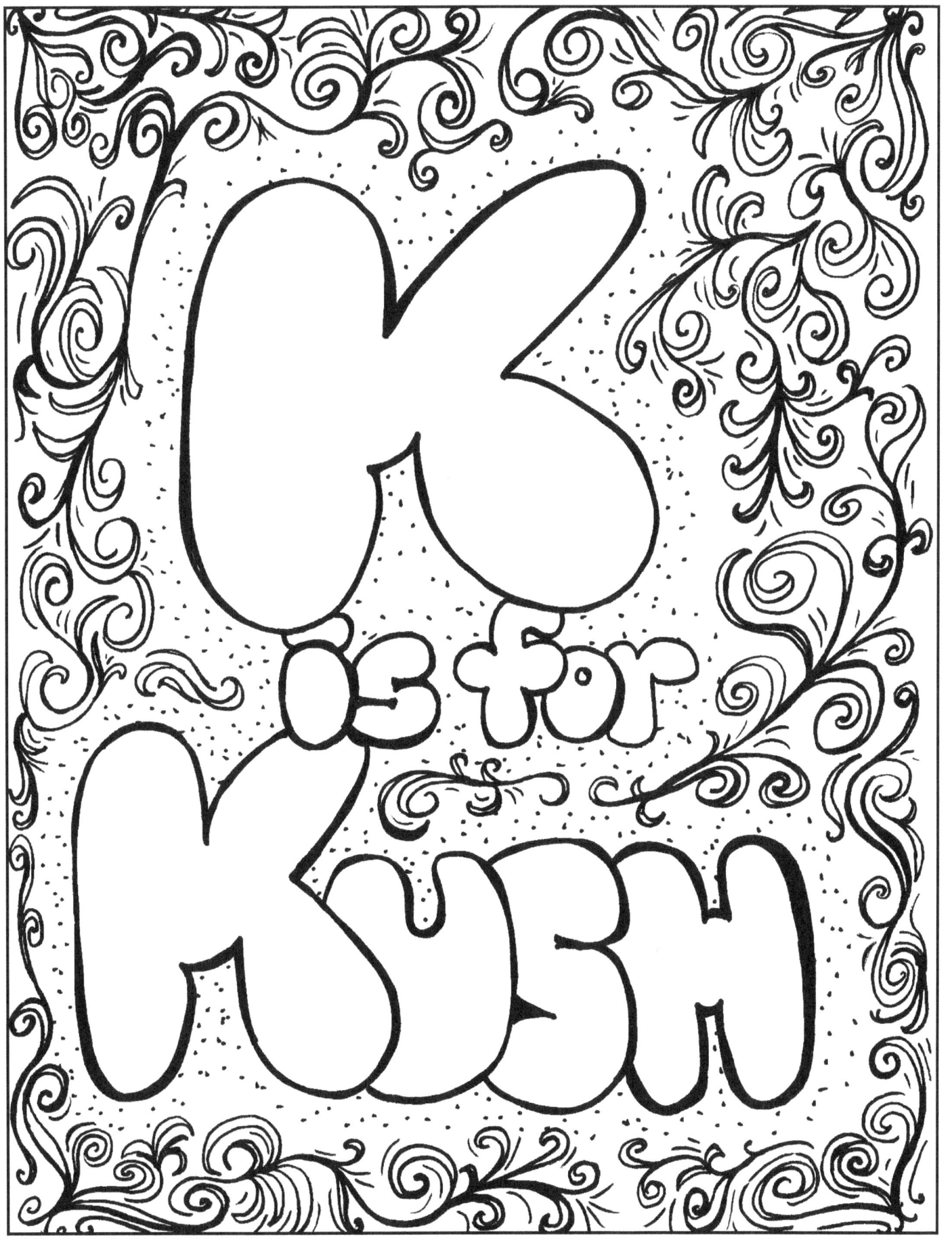

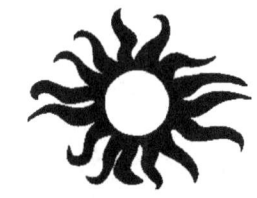

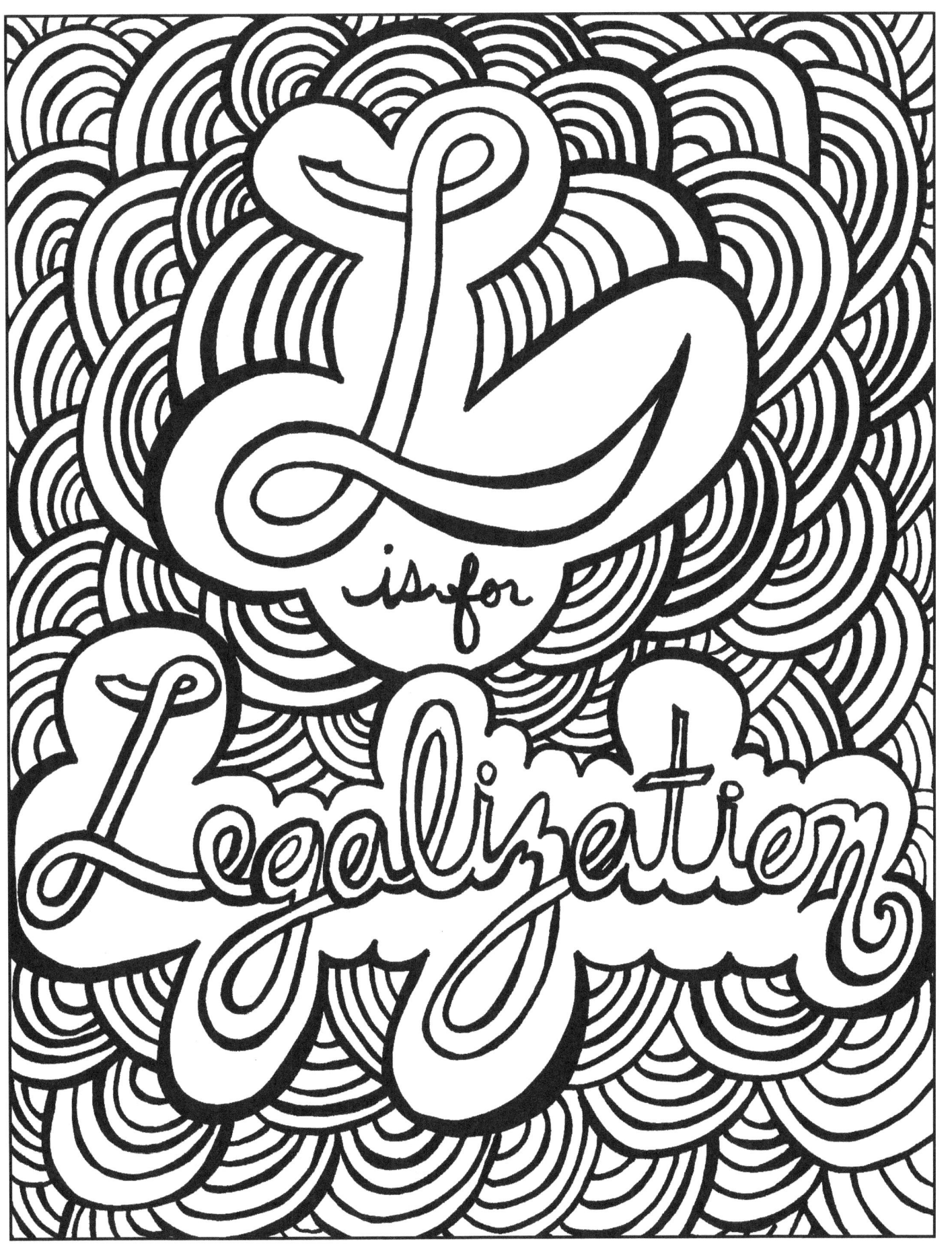

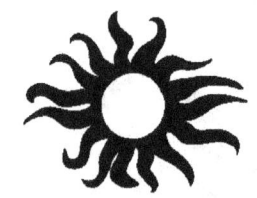

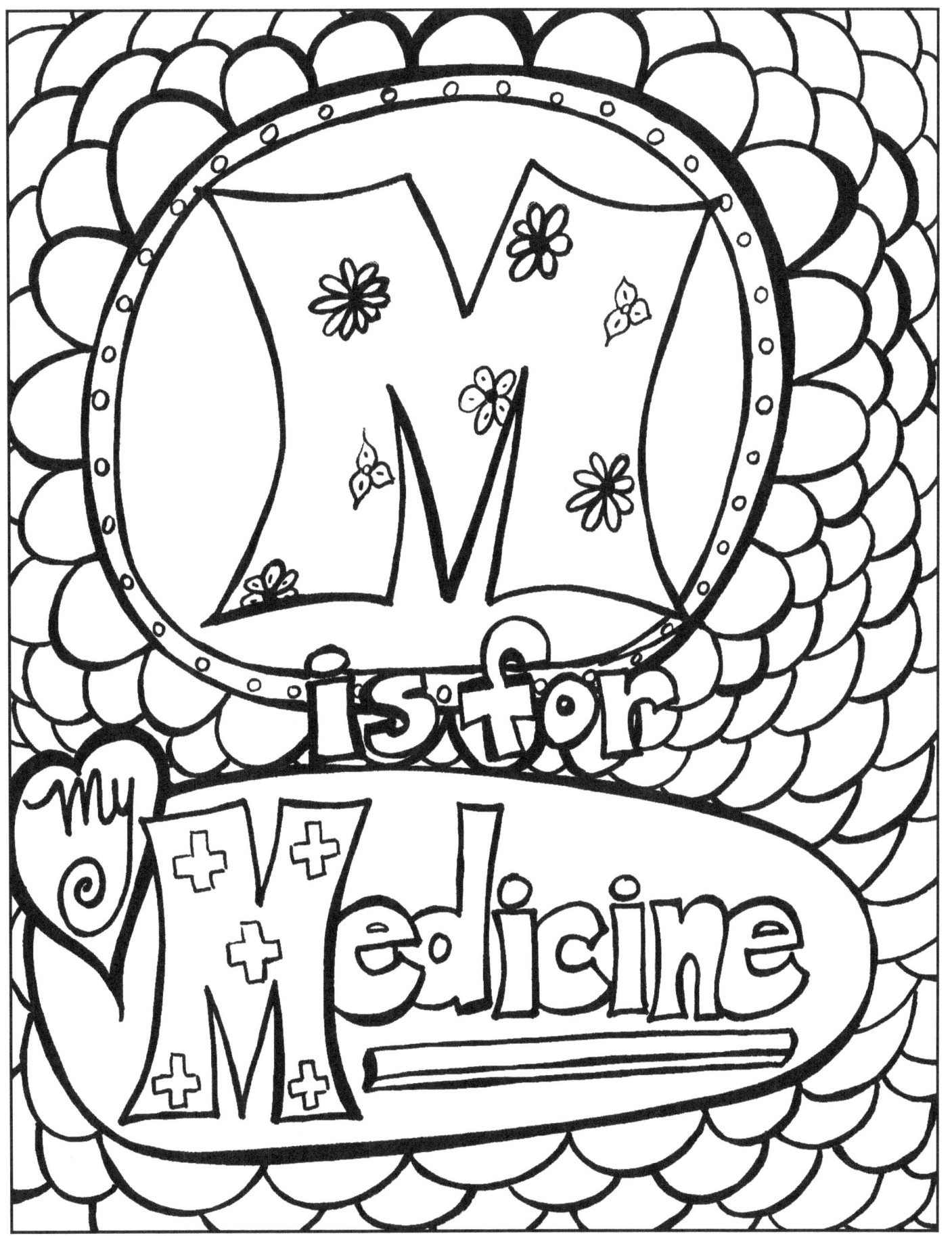

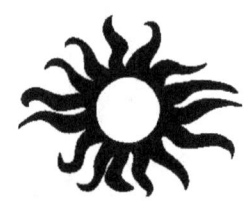

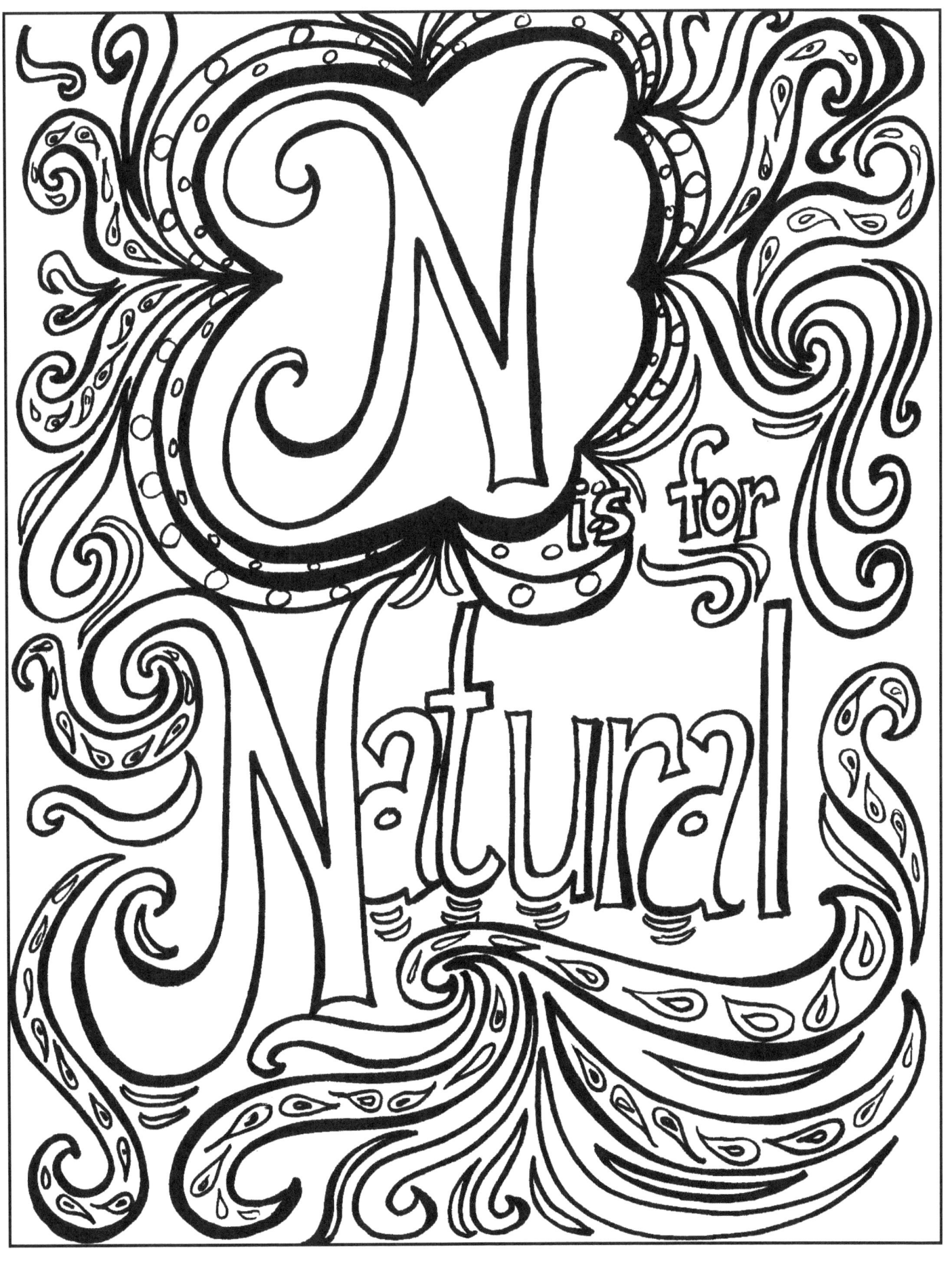

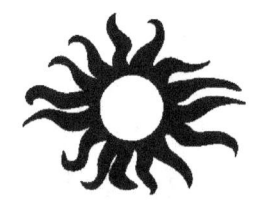

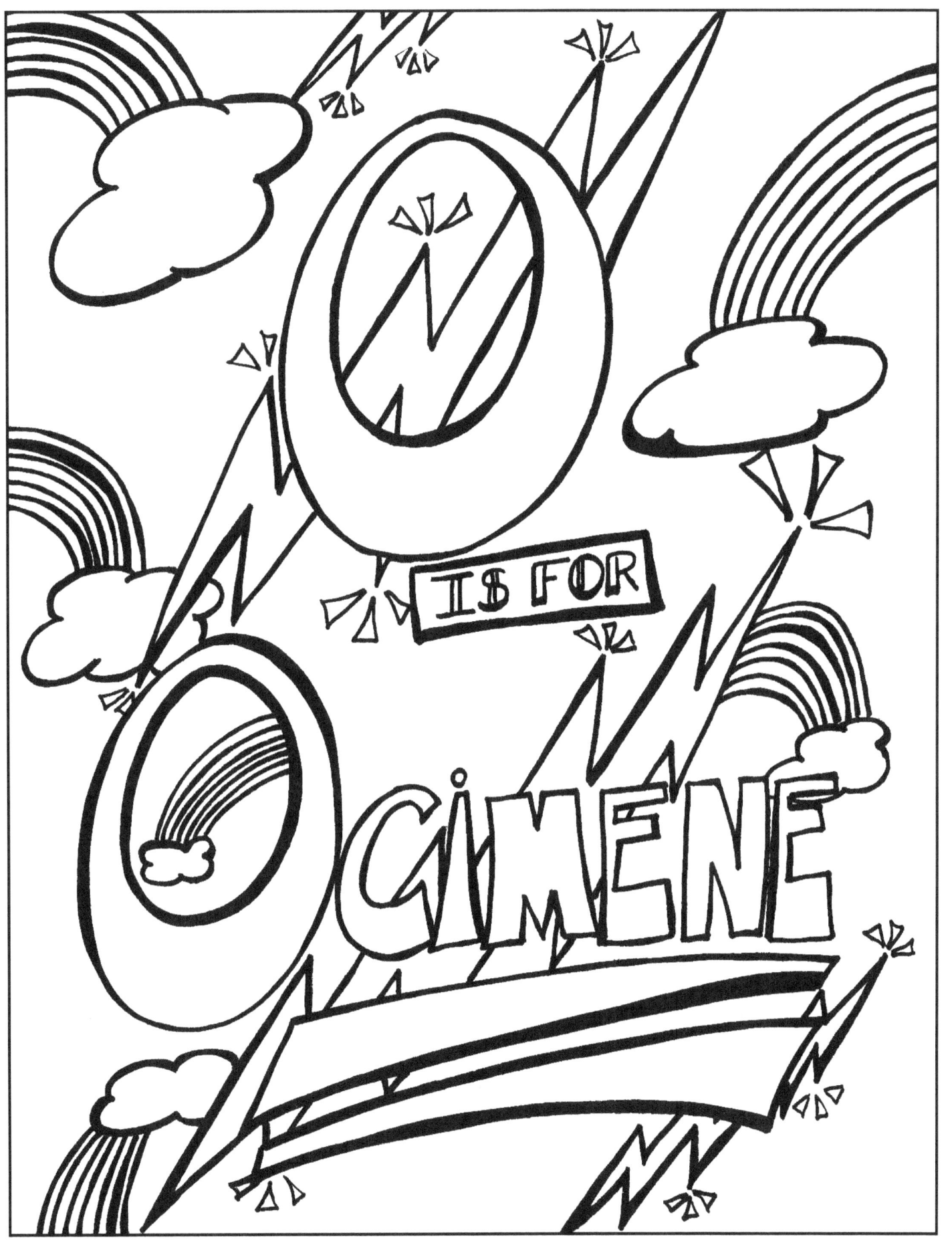
O IS FOR OCIMENE

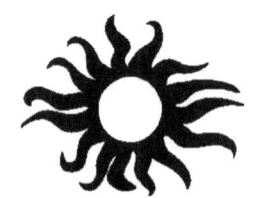

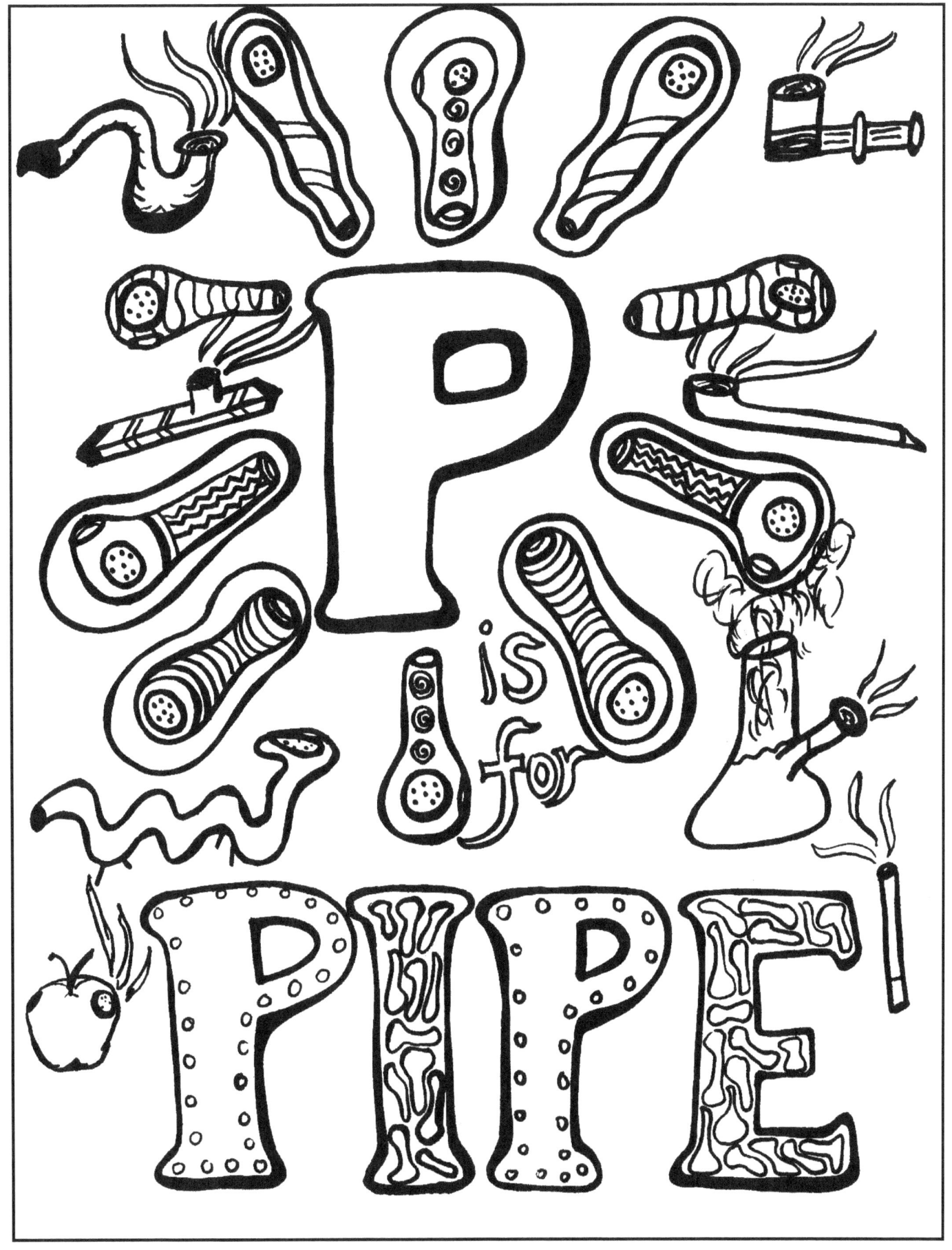

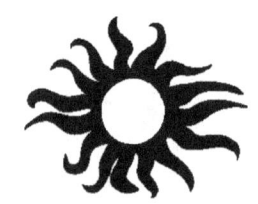

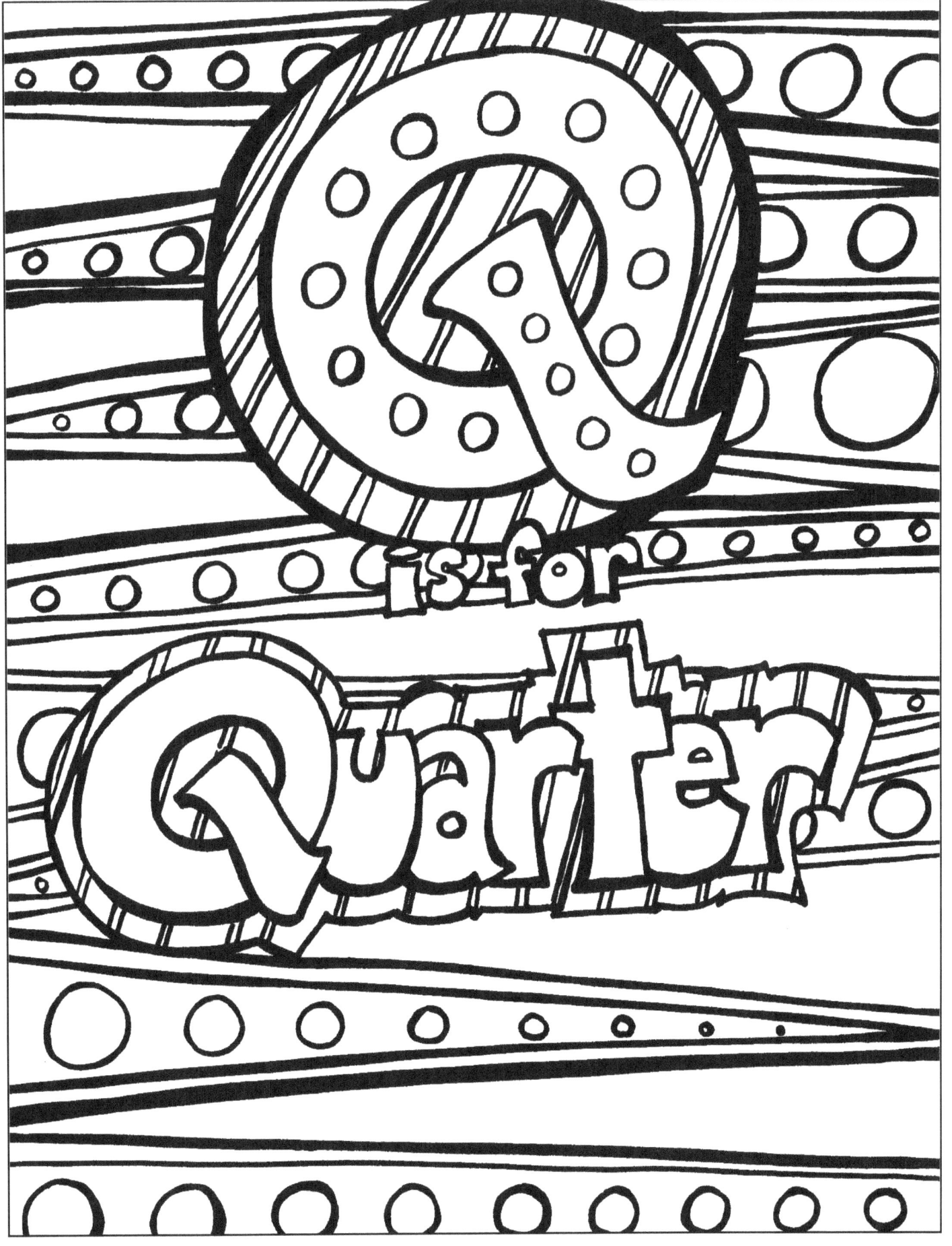

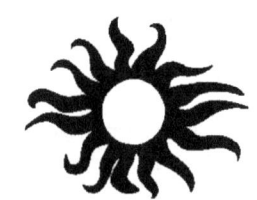

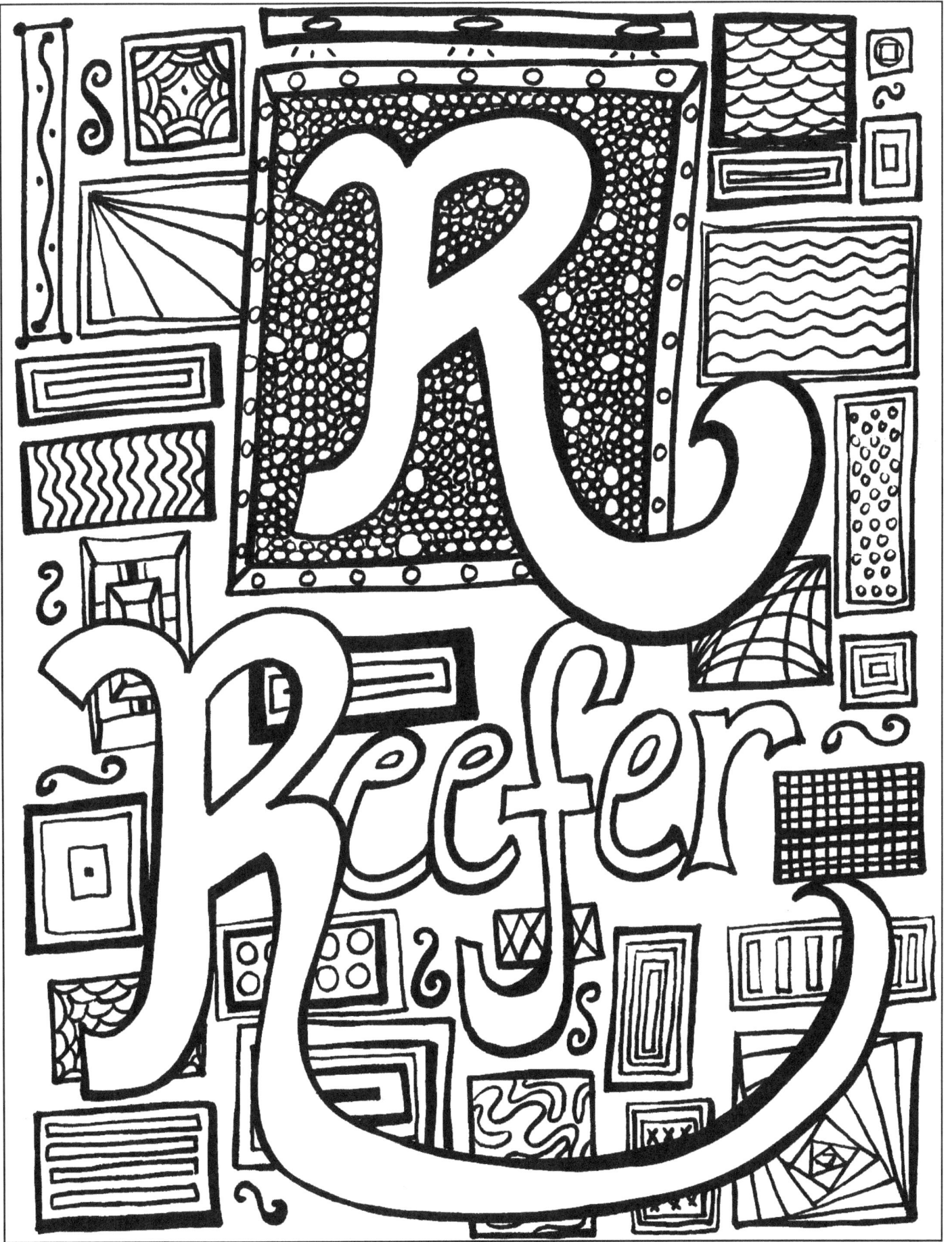

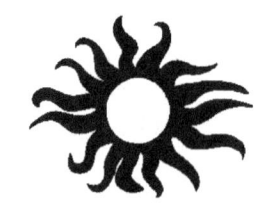

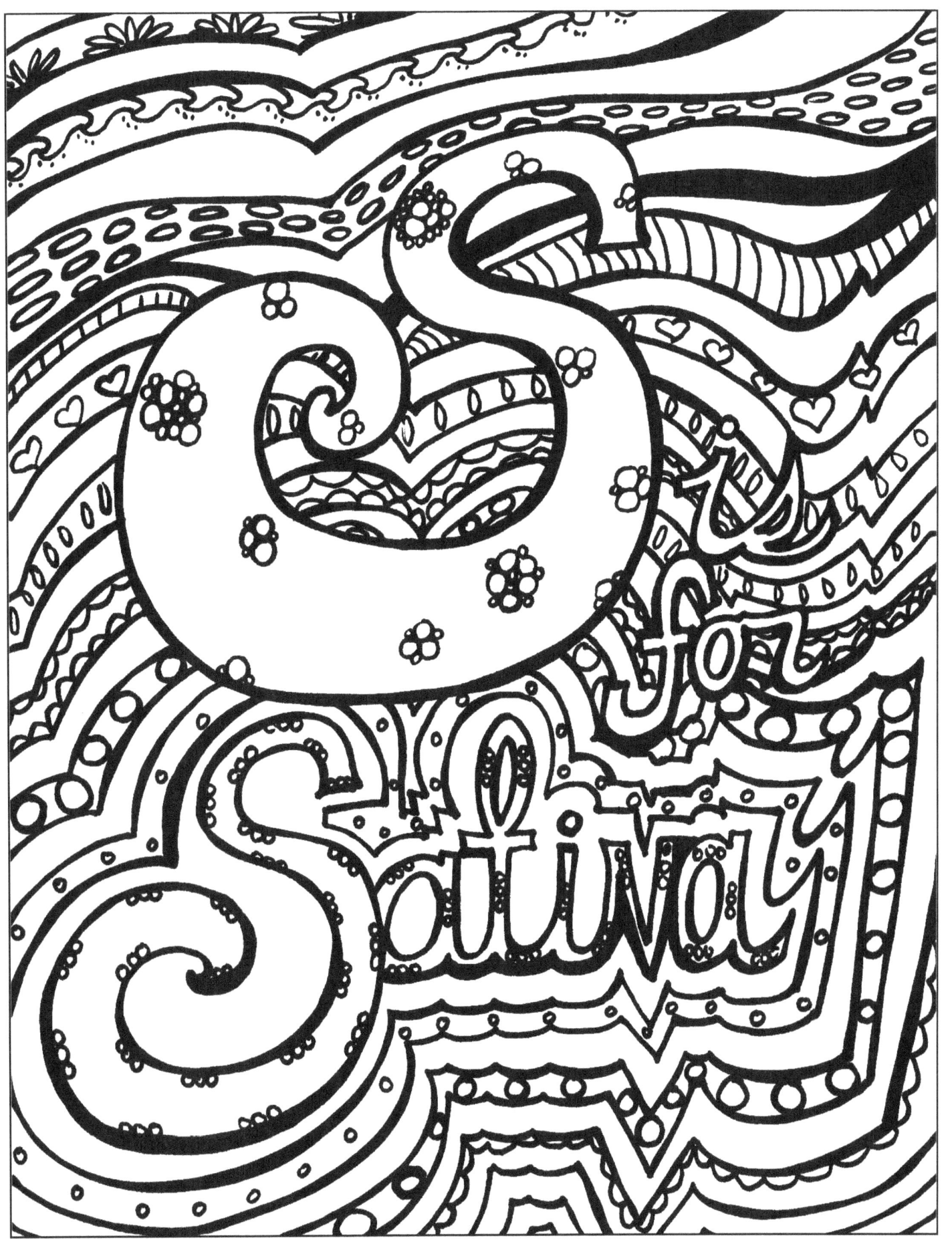

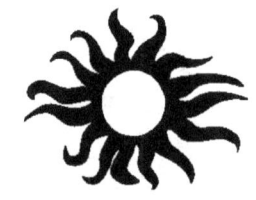

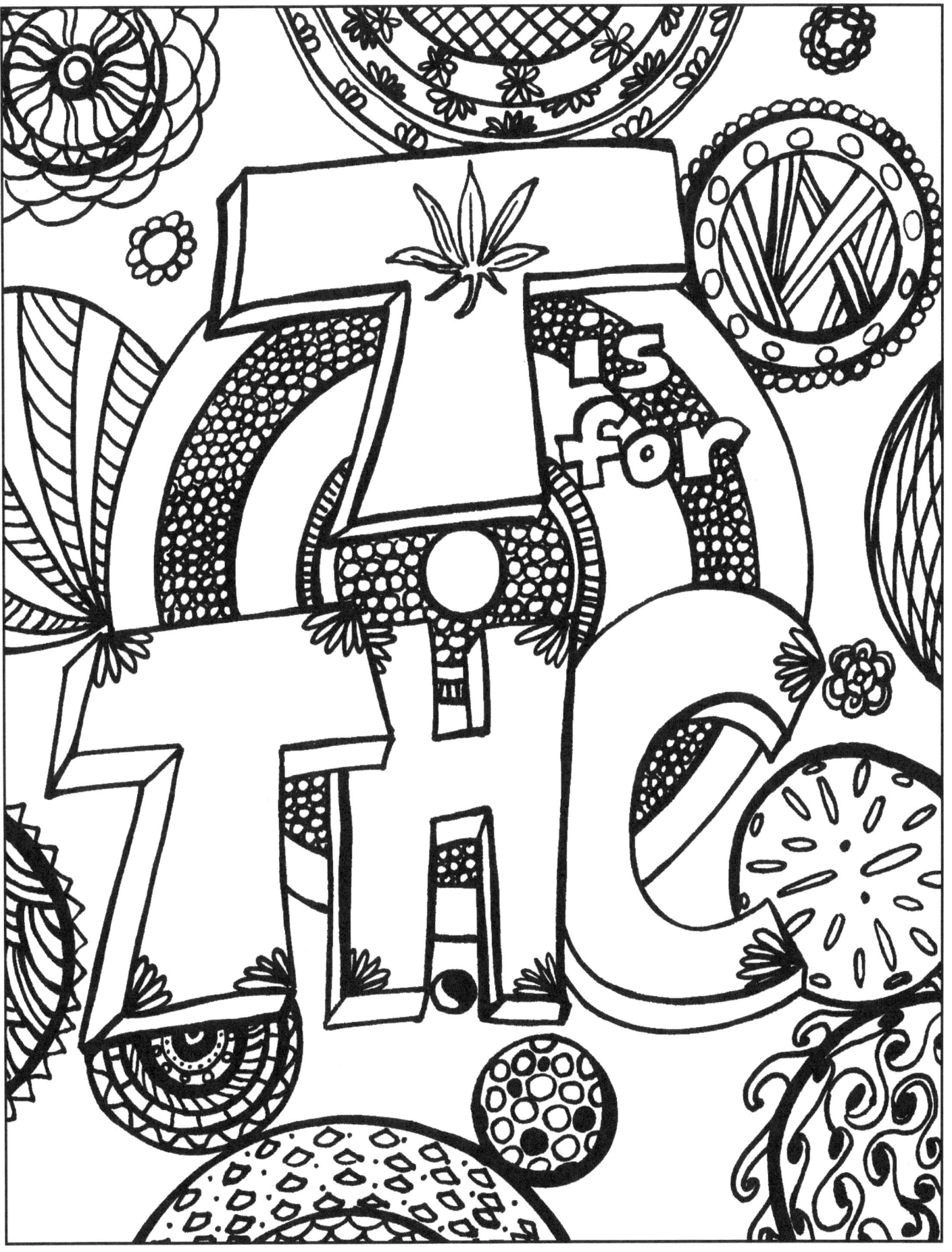

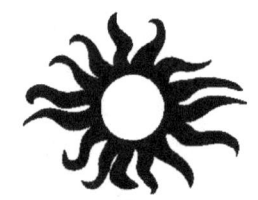

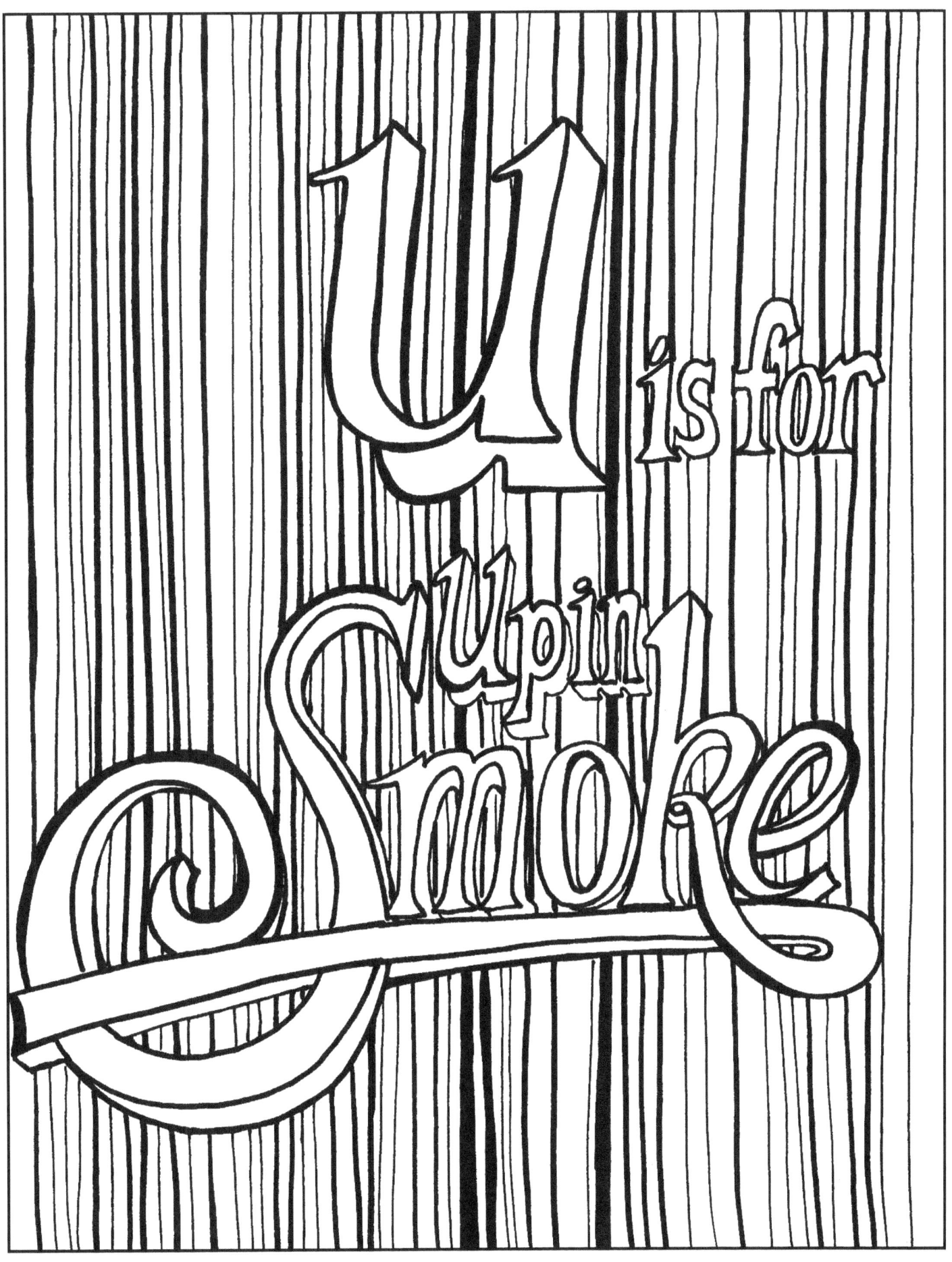

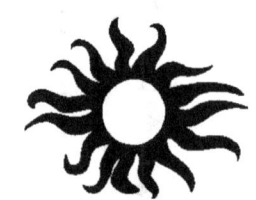

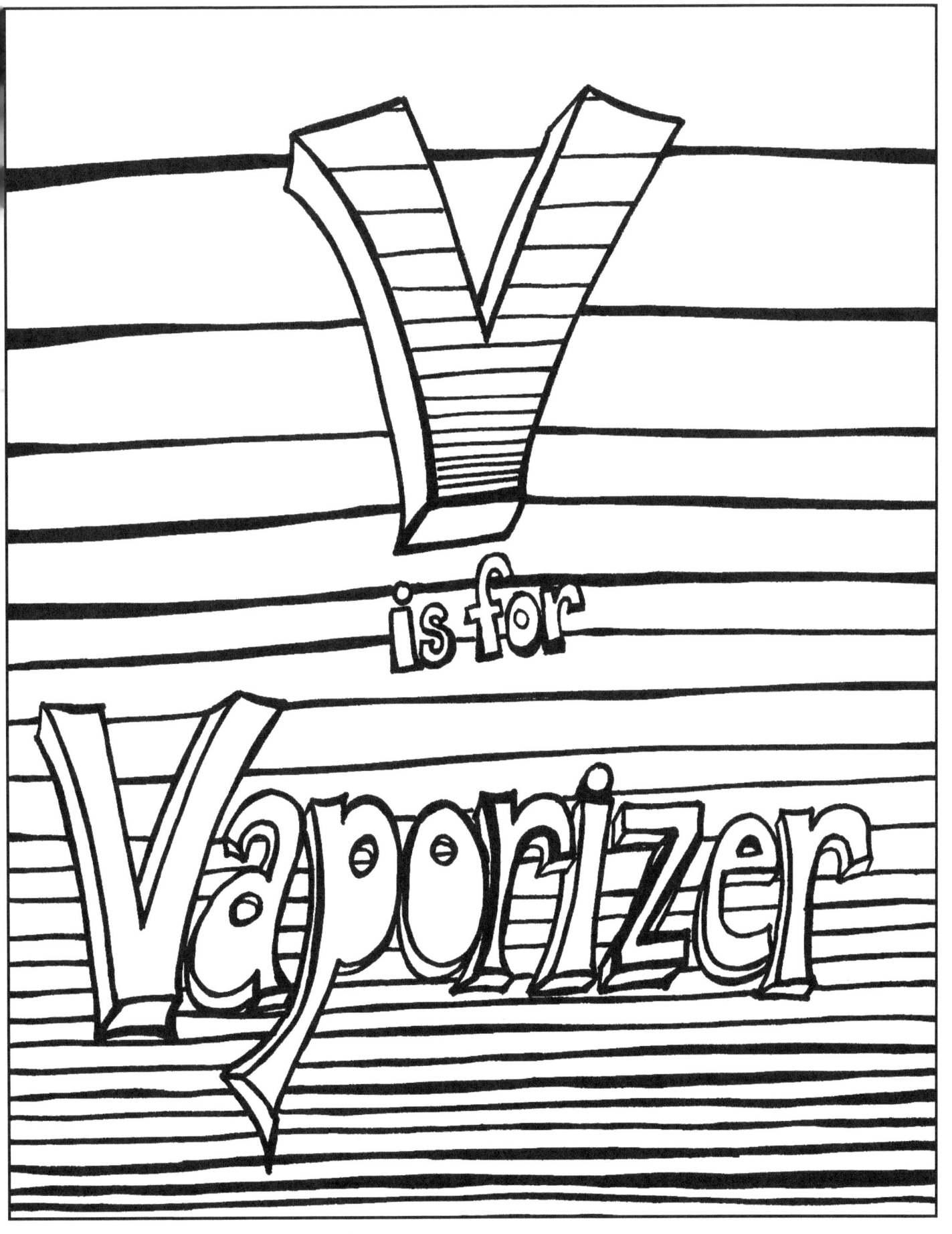

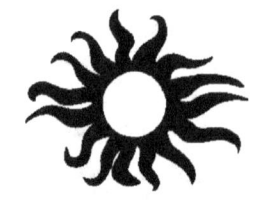

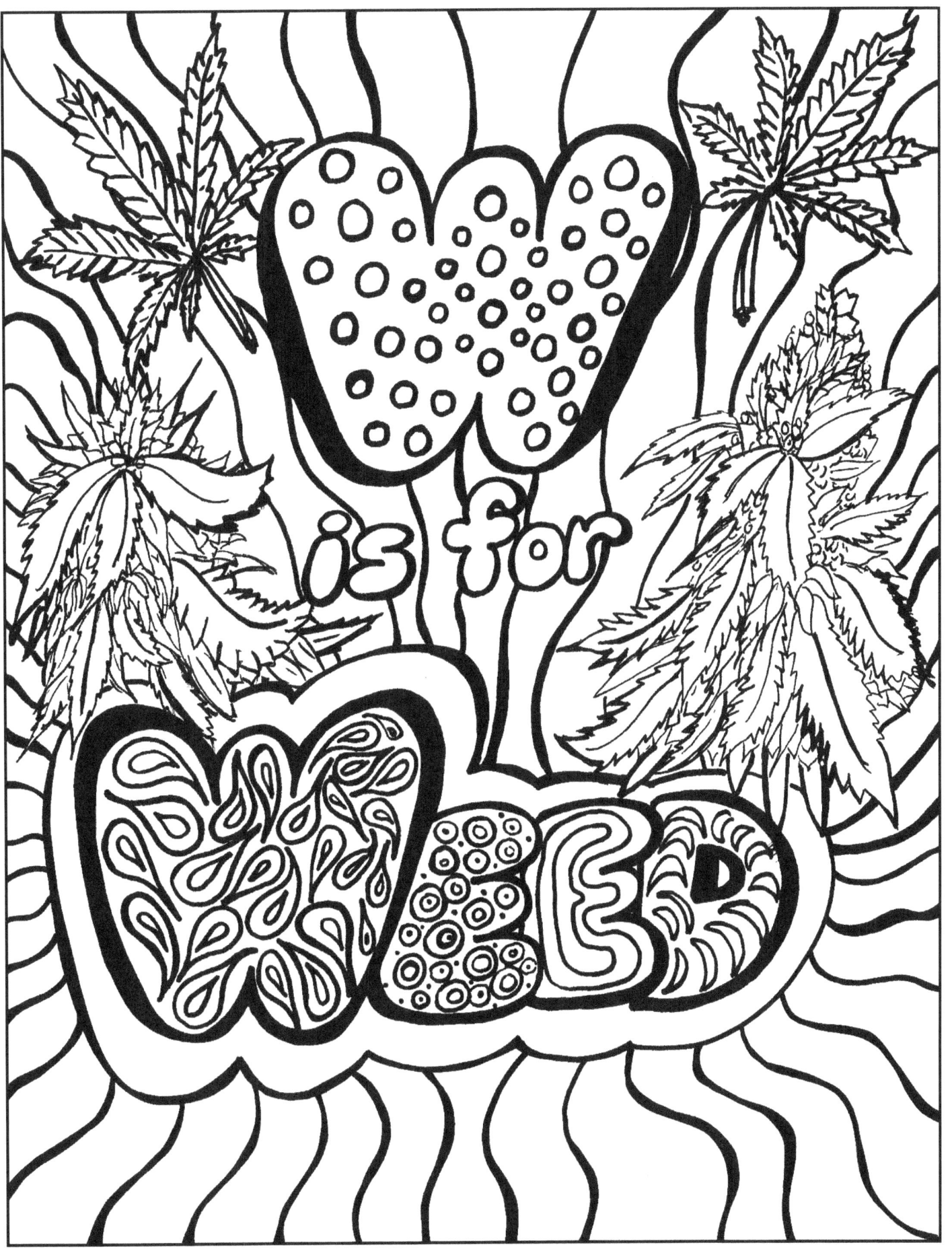

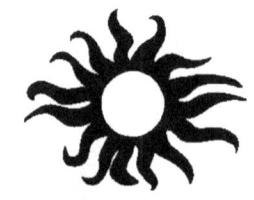

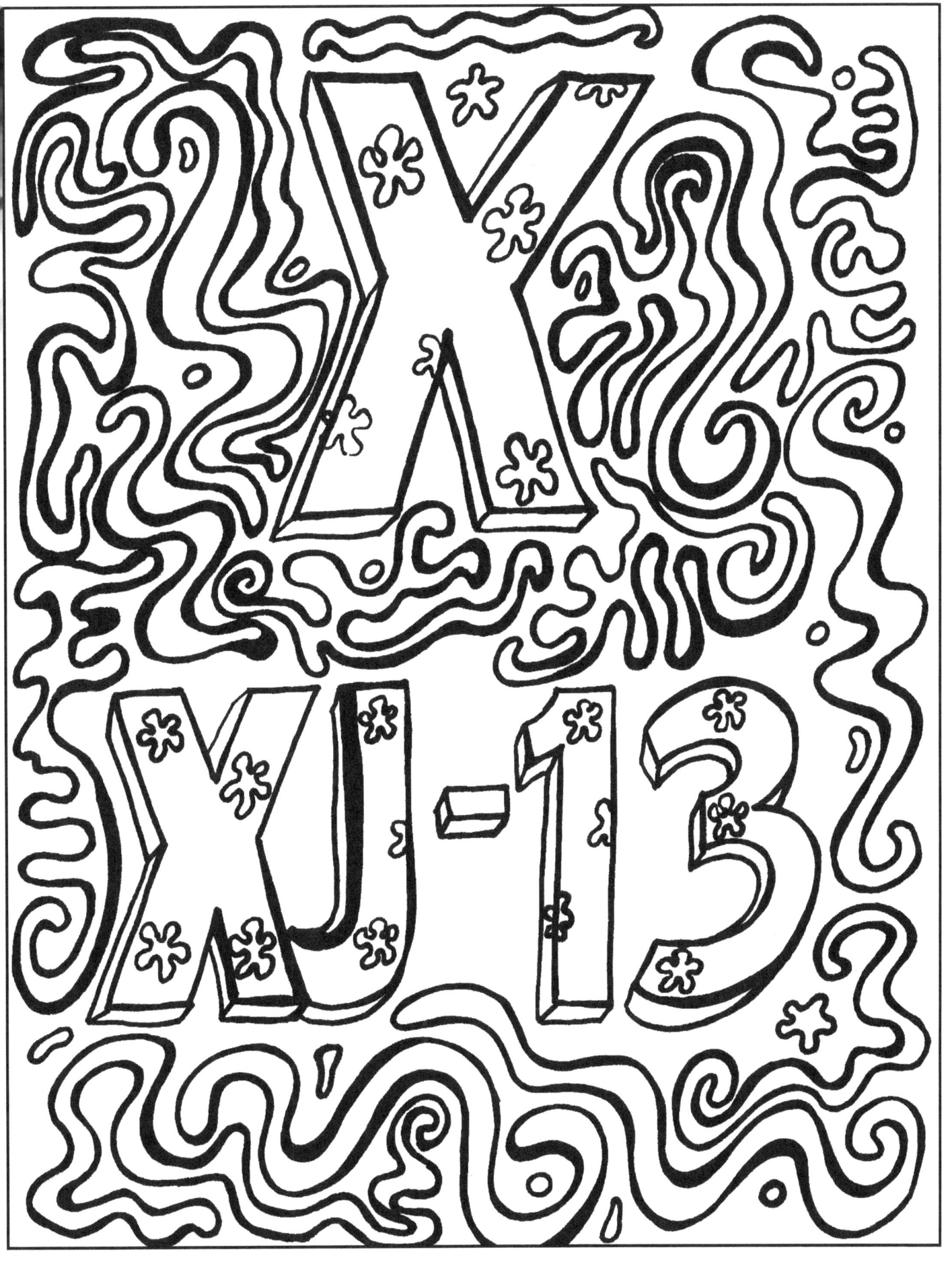

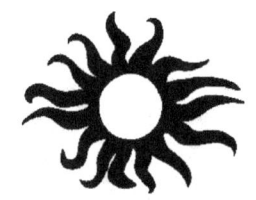

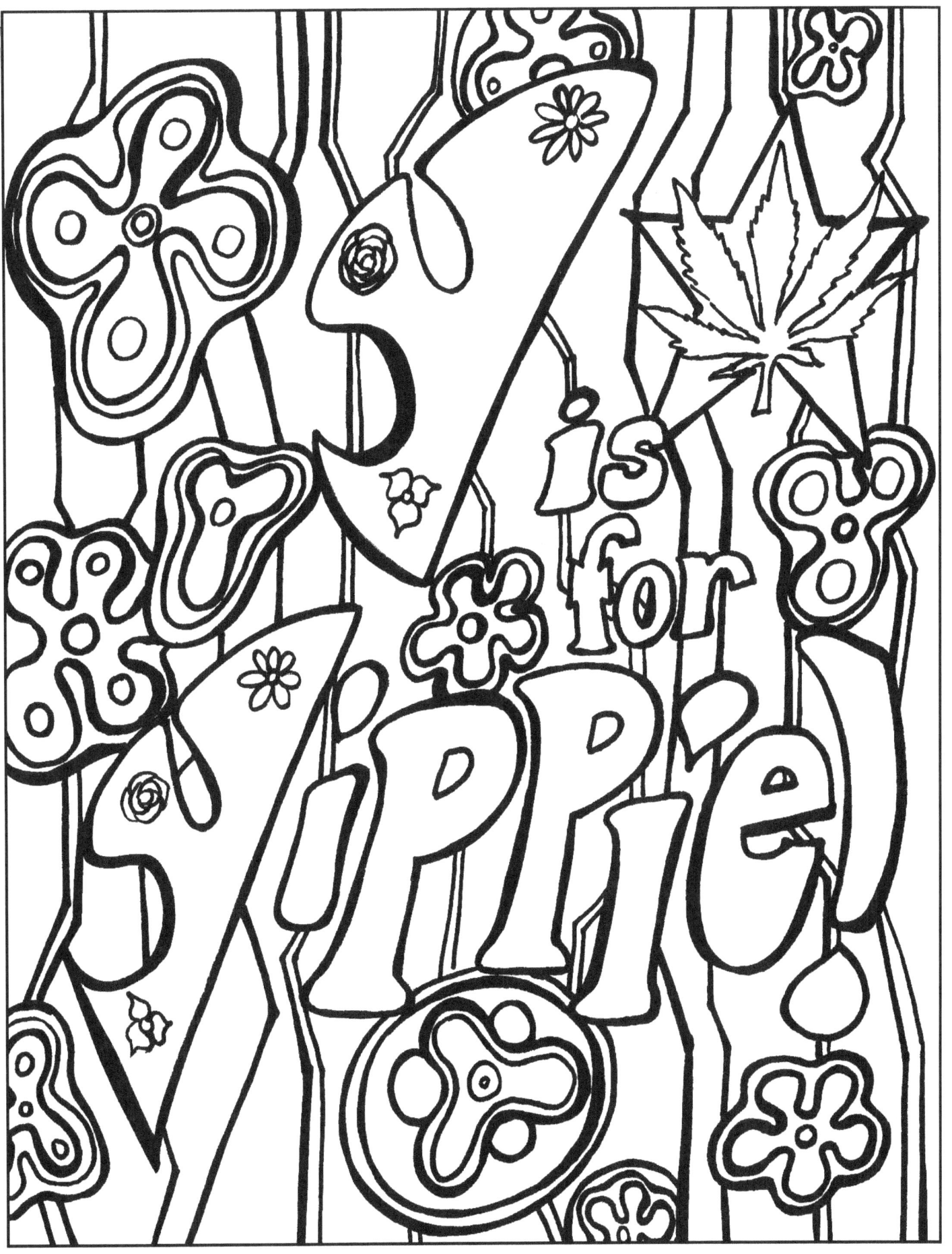

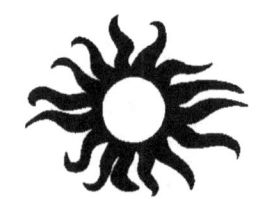

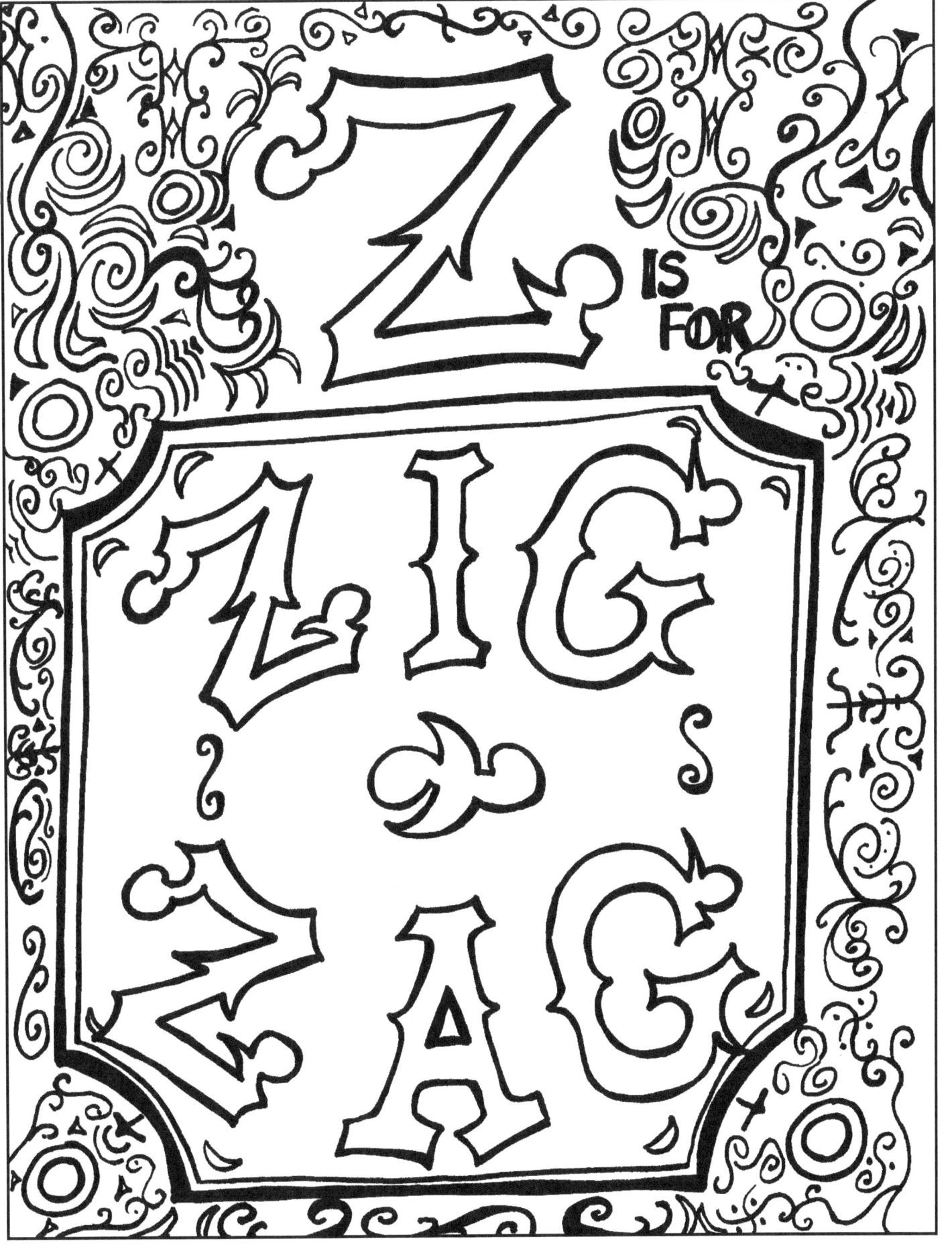

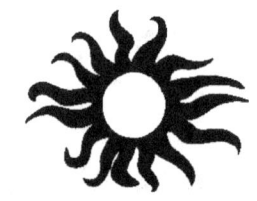

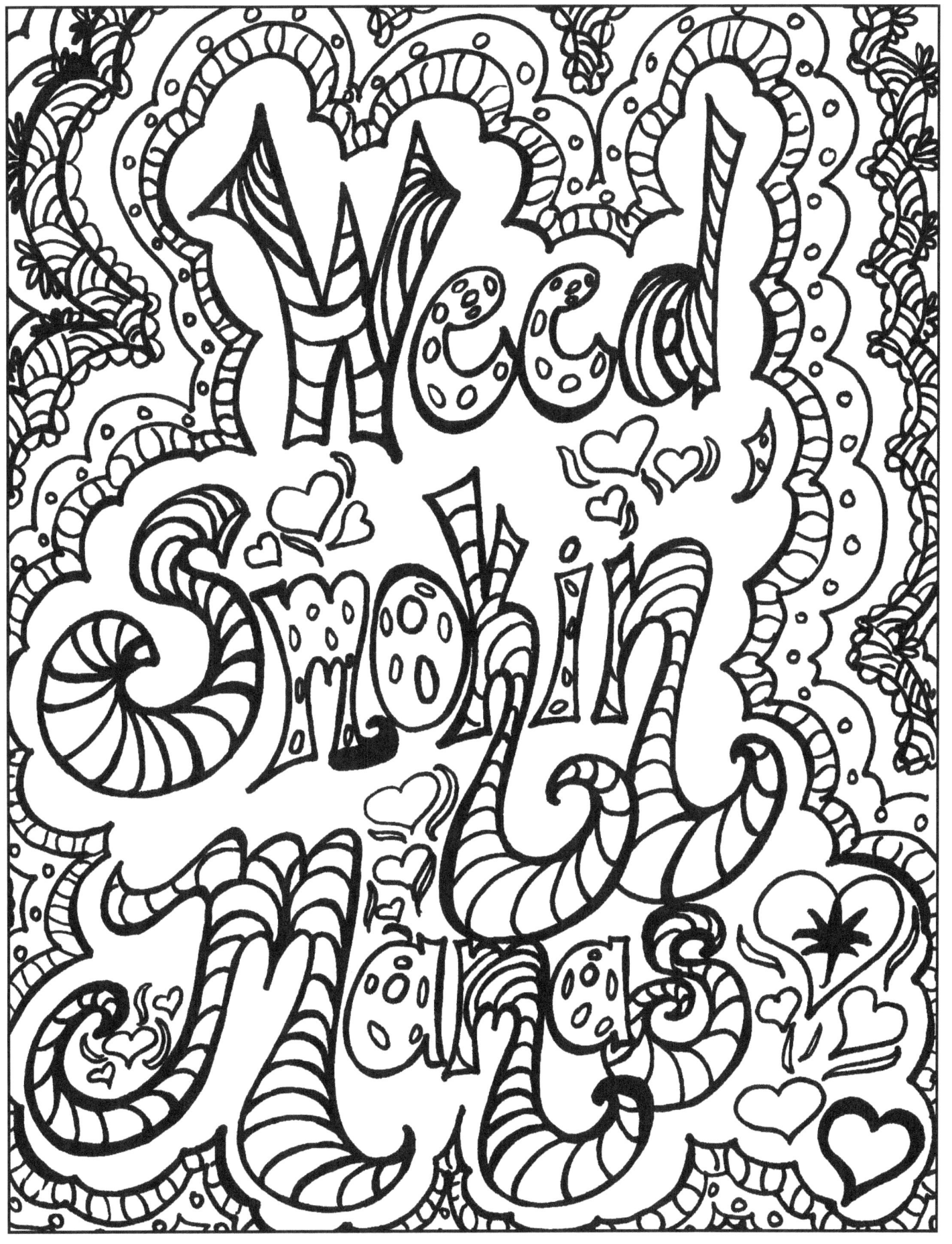

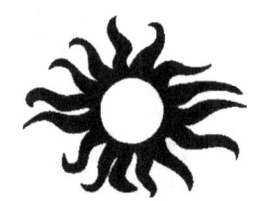

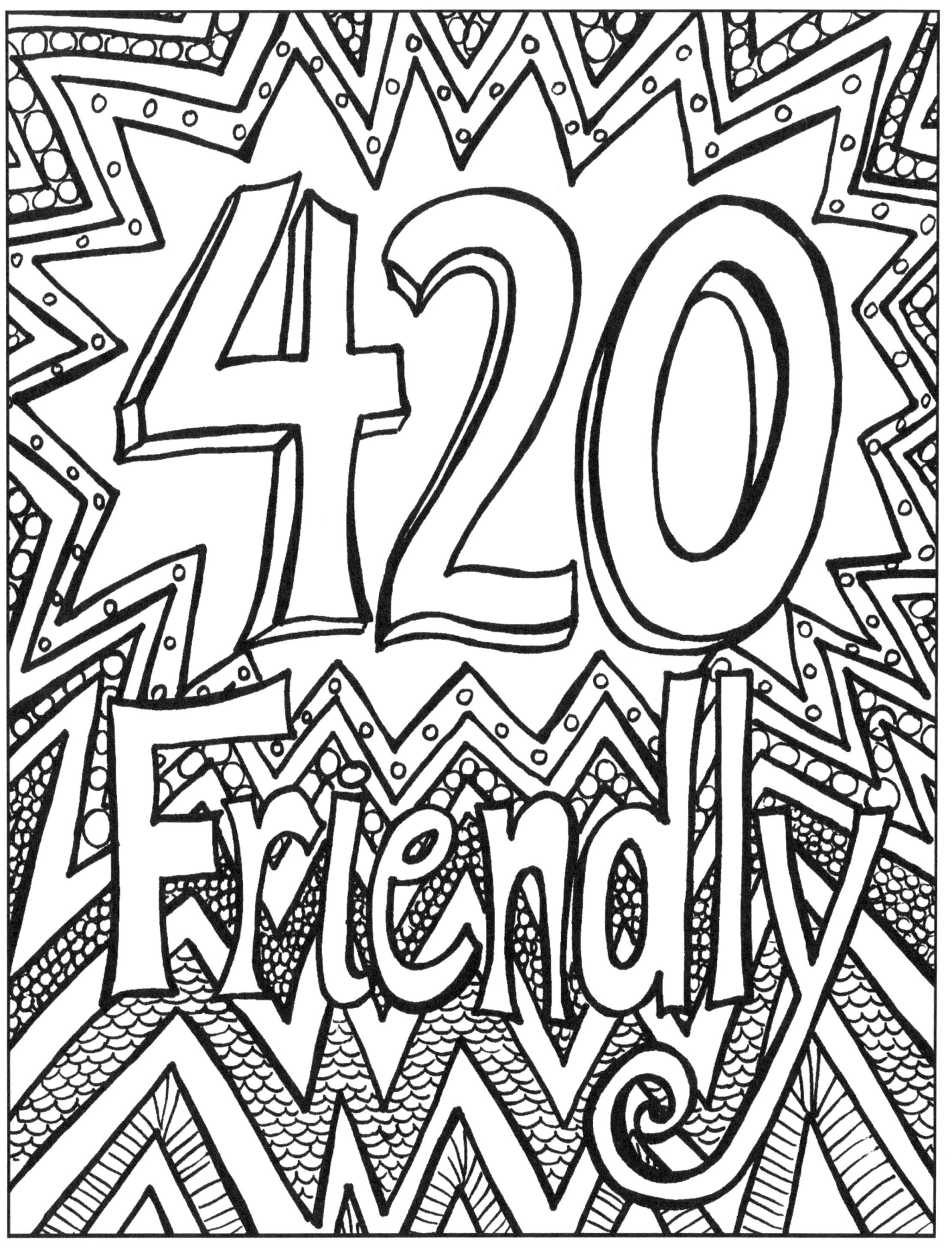

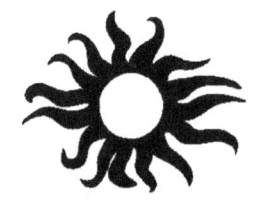

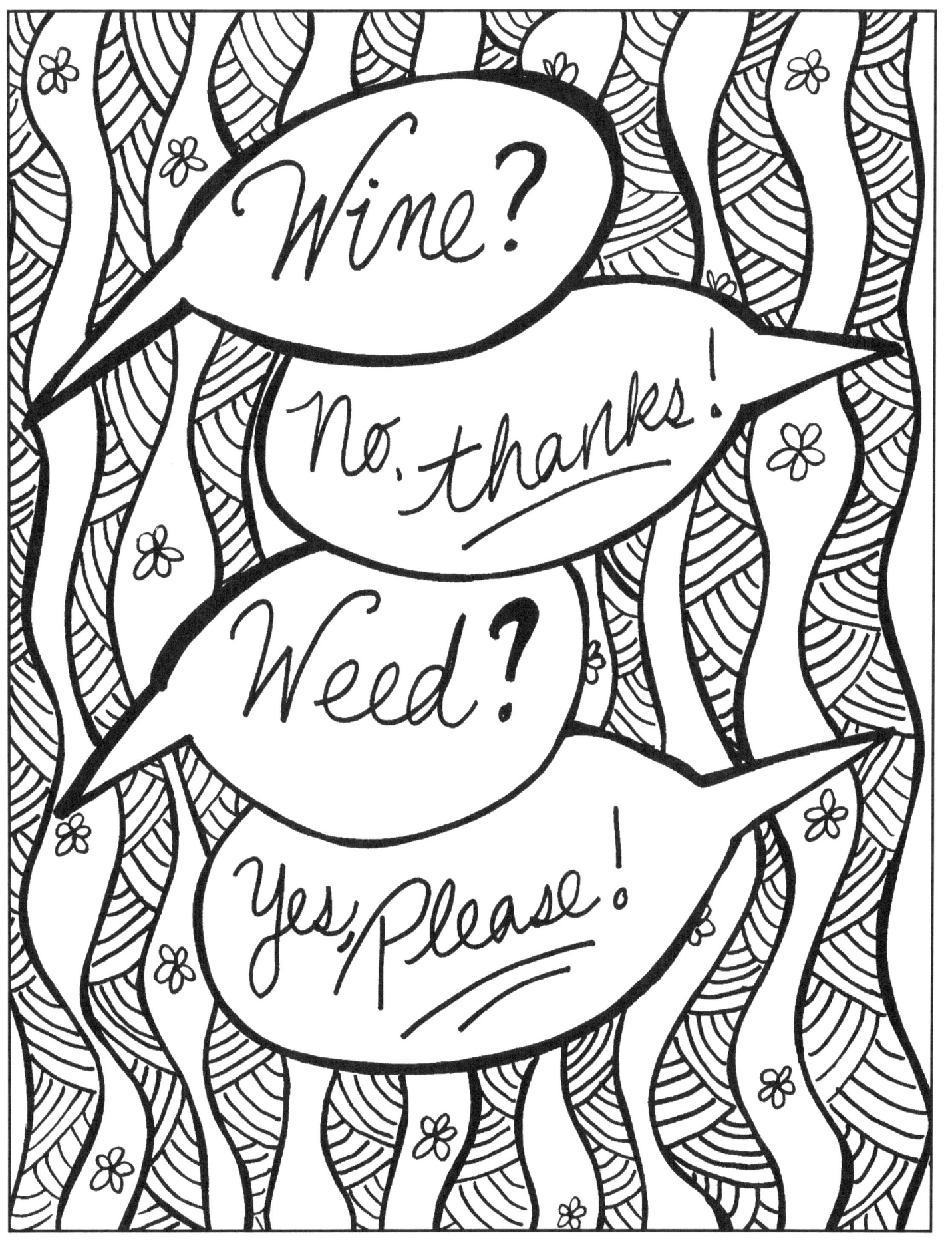

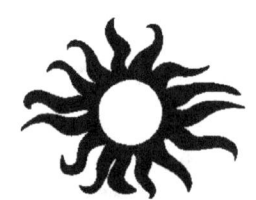